Clues About Jews
for
People Who Aren't

Sidney J. Jacobs, M.A.H.L., D.D.
Betty J. Jacobs, M.A.

JACOBS LADDER PUBLICATIONS
Culver City, California

First Edition

Copyright © 1985 by
Sidney J. Jacobs and Betty J. Jacobs

Second Printing, 1987

Library of Congress Catalog Card Number 85-090337
ISBN 0-933647-00-X

Printed in the United States of America
9 8 7 6 5 4 3 2

Contents

About the Authors

Sidney J. Jacobs, M.A.H.L., D.D., is an ordained rabbi and a professional writer and journalist who has written extensively in Christian, Jewish and secular periodicals and has been a newspaperman and editor in Chicago and Los Angeles. His involvement in ecumenical and interfaith activities and his lectures before church and civic groups have given him expertise in answering questions which are frequently asked about Jews and Judaism. In addition to the present volume, he is the author of *The Jewish Word Book* (1982).

Betty J. Jacobs, M.A., is professor of communications at West Los Angeles College in California. She is a media consultant and a freelance writer who has been the recipient of awards for television writing and production. She served as director of broadcasting for the Chicago Board of Rabbis.

Rabbi and Mrs. Jacobs live in Culver City, California (on the old MGM backlot) with their two dogs, Adam and Dodi, who are about the only ones who have not asked questions about Jews and Judaism.

Preface

Ｗe will be at a party, balancing a plate in one hand and dipping a carrot stick into the salsa with the other, when someone comes up and asks, "Do Jews believe in Jesus?"

We'll be catching our breath after the last of a few dozen loops around the top deck of a cruise ship, when a woman approaches with the announcement, "I heard there was a Jewish chaplain aboard. I'm not Jewish, but my son is engaged to a Jewish girl, and I want to know if he has to convert."

Standing on line with us at the movies, our non-Jewish friend asks our suggestion for an appropriate gift for a Bar Mitzvah.

Everywhere, people who aren't Jewish have been asking questions about people who are.

So, we decided to write this book, a guide through what appears to be a maze of queries about Jews and Judaism, questions asked in public, along with those whispered in private.

The questions and situations posed in the following pages represent an honest attempt on the part of the authors to repeat those most frequently asked of us.

This curiosity is understandable, for Jews are a highly visible and articulate segment of the urban U.S. population. Despite the fact that they constitute only 2.5 percent of the population, Jews in this country are constantly confronting, or being confronted by, persons who are not Jewish in commerce, the professions, media, arts and entertainment.

Even when they are genuinely interested in Jews, their religion and culture, curious individuals who are not Jews are often inhibited from blundering into forbidden byways of cult and customs and are fearful of saying the wrong things or asking the probing questions that might offend and consequently be responsible for terminating a friendship.

We hope that this book will promote understanding by tackling delicate issues together with the "safe" questions.

We want you to bask in the enjoyment of reading this book as much as we did in writing it for you.

—SJJ

—BJJ

Appreciation

W e are immeasurably indebted to many close friends with whom we have discussed various aspects of the subject matter of this book. We express our appreciation and affection to:

Linda J. Byrne, University of West Los Angeles School of Paralegal Studies

William E. Evans, Esq., and Joy E. Evans, Evan-Moor Publishers

Rev. Fr. Sean Brendan Flanagan, St. Catherine of Siena Catholic Church

Leslie D. Tryon Fowler, California Society of Illustrators

Major J. Riley Fowler, Jr., U.S.A.F.

Renée L. Harrangue, Ph.D., Loyola Marymount University

Rev. Wayne C. Hartmire, Jr., United Farm Workers ministry

Harry Hood, La Verne University

Nehama Jacobs, vice-president, Young & Rubicam New York

June E. O'Connor, Ph.D., Department of Religious Studies, University of California, Riverside

Joan Peck, past president, City of Los Angeles Animal Regulation Commission

Philip L. Pick, Jewish Vegetarian Society (London)

Bonnie Remsberg, author and journalist

—SJJ
—BJJ

Authors' Note

In most instances throughout the book, where a Hebrew word is used, it is italicized and followed by a phonetic transliteration, with the accented syllable in upper-case letters. We hope this will make it easier for the reader to pronounce the Hebrew words correctly.

The initials B.C.E. and C.E. are used in identifying dates and periods of time. Since the initials commonly used in reckoning dates, B.C. and A.D., represent "Before Christ" and *"Anno Domini,"* the "year of our Lord," and refer to the birth of Jesus, Jews find it more appropriate to use the initials B.C.E. (Before the Common Era) and C.E. (Common Era).

B.C.E., therefore, identifies the same period as the more familiar B.C. does. C.E. refers to the same time period as A.D.

English translations of verses from the original Hebrew of *The Holy Scriptures* are copyrighted by and used through the courtesy of The Jewish Publication Society of America.

—SJJ
—BJJ

1

Who We Are and Where We Come From

Were Adam and Eve Jewish?

No, not even when they covered their nakedness with fig leaves. Judaism had not come into the world yet, though the Adam and Eve story was to become a part of the account of Creation in the book of Genesis in the Hebrew Bible.

Then, who was the first Jew?

Abraham gets the nomination, because he was the first to perceive monotheism, that there is only One God and not a myriad of pagan gods.

It might be more accurate to describe him as the first Hebrew, since Judaism as we know it today evolved much later.

Abram, as he was first known, was called a Hebrew *(eev-REE)*, which means "one who crossed over" or one "from the other side of the river," because, with his father, Terah, he crossed the river Euphrates from his home town of Ur in Babylonia to Haran in what is now the south of Turkey.

Finally, Abraham crossed over to the land of Canaan—and Jewish history began!

What is the origin of the name, "Jew"?

A portion of ancient Palestine, centered in Jerusalem, was known by the Roman name of Judaea.

People who lived in that part of the Holy Land were known as Judaeans, then as Jews.

Today's Jews are descendants of the ancient Judaeans and the tribe of Judah.

How old is Judaism? When did it begin?

The term, Judaism, was first used by Greek-speaking Jews in the first century.

We can trace the origins of the Jewish religion to the Bible, especially in the formation of monotheism, the belief in One God, and in the ethical and ceremonial laws.

To track the shaping of Judaism in post-Biblical times, we might want to turn back to the fifth century B.C.E. and the Babylonian Exile, when Jews were exiled from Palestine and carried off to Babylonia.

"By the rivers of Babylon, there we sat and wept as we thought of Zion" *(Psalms 137:1),* the captive Hebrews lamented.

It was in Babylonia that the institution of the synagogue most probably came into being, along with the practice of regular public reading of the *Torah (toe-RAH),* the Pentateuch.

You can also trace the age and origin of Judaism to the time, 2,000 years ago, when Rabbi Jochanan ben Zakkai *(yo-khah-NAHN behn ZAH-kai),* fleeing the ruins of the Second Temple in Jerusalem at the hands of the Romans, established a seminary in the nearby town of Yavneh to teach and ordain rabbis. That was in 70 C.E.

This event marked the beginning of what is called Rabbinic Judaism.

Is Judaism the oldest religion?

No. There were pagan, idol-worshipping religions long before Judaism. However, Judaism is the oldest monotheistic religion, professing a belief in One God.

There is a theory which claims that a form of monotheism in ancient Egypt during one of the Pharaonic dynasties preceded Jewish monotheism.

Nevertheless, it is generally conceded that the ancient Hebrew concept of One God endured and was transmitted to the world through Judaism and, later, Christianity and Islam.

Who or what is a Semite?

A member of a people who speak a Semitic language such as Hebrew, Aramaic or Arabic and who, if they trace their roots far back enough, would find them planted in Southwest Asia thousands of years ago.

The name, Semite, comes from Shem, the eldest son of Noah. *(Genesis 5:32)* The Semitic peoples are supposed to be descended from Shem.

Do you mean that the Arabs are Semites?

Yes, the Arabs are Semites, just like the Jews!

On March 3, 1919, the Emir Feisal, then the leader of the Arab world, wrote a letter to Felix Frankfurter (later a justice of the U.S. Supreme Court), who was a leader of American Zionism, in which the former stated, "We feel that the Arabs and Jews are cousins in race, suffering similar oppressions at the hands of powers stronger than themselves..."

It is wrong to call the hostility which many Arabs have for Jewish people since the creation of the State of Israel by the name of "anti-Semitism," since both sides are Semites.

Do Jewish people belong to different tribes?

Not anymore. Dividing Jews up according to tribes became obsolete even before the beginning of Christianity.

Today's Jews are, for the most part, descendants of the tribe of Judah; hence the names Judaea and Jew.

I have heard somewhere that American Indians are part of the Lost Tribes of Israel. Is there any truth to this?

The patriarch Jacob had 12 sons *(Genesis 35:22–26)*, each of whom became the head of a tribe of Israelites bearing his name. Two of the tribes—Judah and Benjamin—made up the southern Kingdom of Judah, later known as Judaea. The other 10 tribes inhabited the northern Kingdom of Israel.

In 722 B.C.E., this northern kingdom fell to the Assyrians, and its inhabitants were exiled *(II Kings 17:6 and 18:11)* and were believed never to have returned to Palestine.

There has been some fascinating speculation but no hard evidence as to what happened to these 10 Lost Tribes. One theory is that they migrated across a land bridge which joined Africa and South America in ancient times and became the Indians of this continent.

People who believe this theory offer as one piece of evidence the idea of the Great Spirit, who is the center of the religion of the American Indians, and who is supposed to resemble *YaHWeH,* the God of the Hebrews.

Put that in your peace pipe and smoke it!

How many Jews are there in the world?

About 13 million now. Six million Jews were killed in the Nazi Holocaust.

How many Jews are there in the United States now?

There are 5.728 million Jews in the U.S., according to the *American Jewish Year Book,* 1984 edition.

That's 2.5 percent of the total population of the United States.

When did Jews first come to the United States? Were there Jews on the Mayflower?

There were no Jews on the ship which brought the Pilgrim Fathers and Mothers across the Atlantic, since the Mayflower manifest consisted of Christians fleeing persecution in England.

However, long before those days, back in 1492, there were Jews who accompanied Columbus on his voyage of discovery to the New World. One of them was Luis de Torres, who is believed to have been the first white man to set foot on this hemisphere. The Jewish astronomer, Abraham Zakuta, was the mapmaker who drew up the nautical tables for Columbus' voyage.

There is a theory which still persists that Christopher Columbus (Cristobal Colon), was himself a Jew, a descendant of Marranos, secret Jews who had to conceal their identities because of the Spanish Inquisition. But that's another story.

Jews first settled in North America in 1654. Twenty-three men, women and children who had left the Netherlands and settled in Brazil, had to leave that country's seaport, Recife (Pernambuco), because the Inquisition followed them.

They landed in Nieuw (New) Amsterdam and asked its governor, Peter Stuyvesant, for permission to settle. At first, he resisted, but after they appealed over his head to the Dutch West Indies Company, he relented.

2

Can You
Tell by Looking?

I've met many Jewish people who don't look Jewish. Don't Jews constitute a race?

Jews are not a true race in the anthropological or ethnological sense. You have only to look around a place where Jews are clustered, a synagogue or a religious school classroom, to note the wide variety of head shapes, hair color, facial features and other external signs of racial "purity."

The so-called "Jewish look" is really a fiction. There are Jews like those who lived until recently in Ethiopia and who are as black as any African tribesmen, and Jews who are as fair-skinned as the Danes with blond hair and blue eyes.

To speak of a "Jewish race" or a "Hebrew race" is an error.

Do Jews have horns?

Strangely enough, your question does come up from time to time, especially by non-Jews who have grown up in small towns where they have never seen a Jewish person. When and if they finally do meet a Jew, they look in vain for horns.

No, Virginia, Jews do not have horns! The image comes from the old myth, common in the folklore of many peoples, that Jews were agents of the Devil; and Satan, or Lucifer, is pictured as having horns. (Ascribing tails to Jews apparently never caught on!)

The myth was given added respectability from the Middle Ages on, when various sculptors portrayed Moses with two horns protruding from his forehead. Michelangelo's statue at San Pietro in Rome is a notable example of a horned Moses, based on the Vulgate, the Latin translation of the Bible in the medieval ages, which mistranslated the Hebrew word for "beams" in *Exodus 34:35* ("sent forth beams") as "horns."

Have you heard the one about the Jewish businessman who visits a synagogue in Tokyo while on a business trip to Japan and is told by a Japanese worshipper at the Jewish Sabbath service there, "You don't look Jewish to me!" Can you tell by looking at someone whether he or she is Jewish?

No way! Originally swarthy, with features like their Arab cousins today, Jews have lived in all parts of the world over the centuries since their dispersion from the Holy Land and have taken on the appearances of many peoples.

There are dark, blonde and red-haired Jews, Jews with round heads, pointy heads, jut-jawed and receding-jawed features, short Jews, tall Jews, skinny Jews, pudgy Jews—all the anthropological characteristics you could conjure.

As for the fabled "Jewish nose," it isn't Hebraic in origin but Hittite (Asia Minor and Syria, 1900 to 1200 B.C.E.).

By the way, there *has* been some interest in Judaism among Japanese intellectuals in recent years. One of them was converted to Judaism after having had himself circumcised as an adult.

A black woman I met wears a Star of David around her neck and told me she is Jewish. I said she must be pulling my leg, but she insisted. Blacks can't be Jewish, can they?

Of course they can, provided they go through the same procedure of studying and converting to Judaism that any person born a non-Jew would.

The only born Jews among blacks in this country would be the children of black mothers (or fathers, in Reform Judaism) who had previously been converted to Judaism.

The *Falashas (fah-LAH-shahs)*—the word means "landless" or "exiled" strangers, and they prefer to be called *Beta Yisrael (BAY-tah yihs-rah-AYL)*—are the Black Jews of Ethiopia. After having lived, and many died, in conditions of persecution and starvation in Ethiopia, most of the *Beta Yisrael* were rescued and brought in 1984 and 1985 to Israel, where they are accepted as Jews.

In the United States, there are some black people who claim to be Jews without having undergone formal conversion. They maintain synagogues in New York City and in Chicago under the leadership of their own "rabbis." Their status, however, is in dispute in Jewish religious circles, since they can neither prove a relationship with the *Beta Yisrael,* nor have they been converted to Judaism.

Are there any Oriental Jews?

There are Jews who live in Oriental countries but who are of Eastern European (Ashkenazic) or Middle Eastern (Sephardic) origin.

Shanghai, the Chinese port city in Kiangsu province, is a good example. In the middle of the 19th century, it was home to very well known Sephardic families from Cairo, Baghdad and Bombay, including the Sassoon family.

The approximately 700 Jews in Shanghai at the time of World War I rose to 25,000 with Russian Jews who left that country after the 1917 revolution, and to 40,000 between 1932 and the outbreak of World War II by refugees from Germany and Nazi-occupied lands.

After suffering under the Japanese occupation, almost all of the Jews in Shanghai left after the war for the United States and Israel.

More than 1,000 years ago, however, during the T'ang dynasty, Jews lived in China. They built a synagogue at K'aifeng in Honan province, half-way between Peking and Shanghai. Many married Chinese women, and their descendants are Chinese, some of whom retain memories of their Jewish antecedents to this day.

3

What Jews Believe

Are there any Jewish saints?

In Judaism, the saints aren't marching in. We don't have anything similar to the church's pantheon of exceptionally holy persons who enjoy a special position in heaven and have been canonized.

In Jewish folklore, there are 36 Righteous Ones upon whose existence the world depends for its survival.

According to this tradition, a Righteous One (called a *LAH-mehd VUHV-nik* for the Hebrew letters having the value of 36) doesn't know that he or she is one. Upon the death of a Righteous One, another is born at once to keep the balance of 36 intact.

However, the Righteous Ones are not the equivalent of the Christian category of saints.

Are there Jewish angels?

The Bible makes many references to angels. It is not always clear whether human or supernatural beings are being written about. These angels are always described as messengers of God, and, sometimes, the angel is God.

Jews believed in angels in the periods after the Bible, including the time of the Talmud. The traditional Jewish prayerbook, to this day, includes references to angels, although most Orthodox Jews view the idea of angels as purely symbolic. Reform and Conservative Jews have eliminated the idea of angels completely.

Poetic reference is still made, however, among all Jewish denominations to the Sabbath Angels, who are welcomed at sunset on Fridays, and to the Angel of Death, a kind of Jewish version of the Grim Reaper.

Is there a Jewish version of a nun?

Nun whatsoever...unless Hollywood produces a movie about a woman religious who kicks the habit to become "Yentl the Trappist Monk."

Do Jews believe in the devil?

The idea of the devil does not occupy the role in Judaism that it does in mainstream Christianity. You will never hear a rabbi portraying his one-on-one conflict with the Devil as you might hear a fire-and-brimstone evangelist preaching of his personal crusade against the Prince of Darkness.

Satan (sah-TAHN), the Hebrew word for devil, has been incorporated into the English language. In Judaism, Satan is conceived as an accusing spirit, a kind of prosecuting attorney, rather than as a demon with horns and forked tail who gleefully entraps people into sin for which they are consigned to the fiery pit of Hell.

What is the Jewish concept of sin?

The Hebrew verb, *khah-TAH,* which means "to sin," also means "to miss," as an archer misses the bull's-eye target.

In the Jewish view, then, sin is "missing the mark," failing to attain one's maximum potential in establishing ethical relationships between living creatures and with the environment.

Repenting of sin is a very important principle as well as an attainable goal in Judaism. Judaism asserts that in the place where a repentant sinner stands even a person who has never sinned cannot stand.

So, if you sin and really, sincerely repent, you can still score high.

On the most solemn and sacred day in the Jewish religious calendar, *Yom Kippur (yome kih-POOR),* the Day of Atonement, Jews spend 24 hours fasting, contemplating personal sins and dealing with the necessity for repentance.

By the way, the concept of Original Sin, the inclination to sin which Christian theology views as an inherent part of human nature ever since the fall of Adam in the Garden of Eden, plays no part in Judaism whatsoever.

Do you have confession and penance?

The procedure of confession as it is known in the church is not a part of Judaism, but the *concept* of confession has been important in the Jewish religion as far back as Bible days. A person "who confesses and gives [faults] up will find mercy." *(Proverbs 28:13).*

Judaism is unique in that it provides for collective or social confession. "For the sins *we* have sinned before You" is a formula frequently repeated in the liturgy of confession. "You" refers to God; Jews do not confess to or through a rabbi or any other intermediary but directly to God.

An entire 24-hour period is set aside each year for taking inventory of one's sins and asking divine forgiveness. This is *Yom Kippur (yome kih-POOR),* the Day of Atonement.

Confession by a dying person is also important. It may be made directly by one who is about to pass away or with the aid of another.

Penance, the Roman Catholic sacrament of confession followed by forgiveness, does not exist in that form among Jews. In the Day of Atonement ritual, the Jew is taught that "Repentance, Prayer and Charity temper the severe decree" on the person who has sinned.

Can Jews be excommunicated?

Excommunication, banishment and isolation from Hebrew or Jewish society for heresy, is mentioned early in the Bible *(Exodus 22:19; Numbers 12:14)* and was provided for and practiced in the Talmud and in post-Talmudic Jewish law.

In modern times, the use of excommunication as a device by extreme Orthodox authorities as a punishment for non-conformity has become meaningless.

Reform and Conservative Jews have neither accepted nor practiced excommunication.

I am a Methodist. To belong to my church and most denominations, Protestants have to affirm a creed. Are Jews mandated to confess a Jewish creed?

No. Judaism requires neither confession nor affirmation of a set creed.

Then, what makes a person Jewish?

One of two facts: being born a Jew or converting to Judaism.

Being born a Jew means, according to *Halacha (hah-LAH-khah)*, Orthodox Jewish guidelines, that your mother is Jewish. In Orthodox and Conservative Judaism, the line of descent is maternal; a person born to a Jewish father and a non-Jewish mother is not considered to be Jewish.

In very recent years, Reform Judaism has begun to recognize the patrilineal (paternal) line of descent as equally valid. In Reform Judaism, therefore, a person having either a Jewish mother or father is considered Jewish.

A person can convert to Judaism by conferring with a rabbi, arranging for a course of study and participating in a conversion ceremony. This presents no problem unless the convert moves to the State of Israel. Orthodox Jewish authorities there, who have control over matters of personal status such as marriage and divorce, insist that for one who has not been born a Jew to be accepted into Judaism he or she must have undergone a conversion procedure supervised by three Orthodox rabbis.

The Orthodox rabbinate will not honor conversions presided over anywhere in the world by Conservative, Reform or Reconstructionist rabbis.

The "Who Is a Jew" debate has been a volatile one in Israel for many years, and the matter still has not been settled.

What are the differences between Reform, Conservative and Orthodox Judaism?

Until the early part of the 19th century, there was only one expression of Jewish religion, that which we today call Orthodox Judaism.

Orthodoxy, which means "the right way," is fundamentalist Judaism. It accepts completely, and will not concede any possibility of change, the Pentateuch as God's word revealed to Moses and the rest of the Hebrew Bible as divinely commissioned.

Further, Orthodox Judaism looks for its authority and sanction to the Talmud with its codifications and other interpretations of *Halacha (hah-LAH-chah)*, rabbinic law.

Strict observance of the Jewish Sabbath, holydays and the dietary laws are characteristic of Orthodox Judaism.

Worship services in Orthodox synagogues are conducted almost exclusively in the Hebrew language and from the traditional prayer book.

Women are segregated from male worshippers in such synagogues and are not qualified to be counted in a *minyan (MIHN-yahn)*, the quorum of 10 necessary to hold a religious service.

Heads are covered, and prayer shawls are worn by the men at services. Neither organ nor other instrumental music is permitted during worship.

Reform Judaism came into existence in Germany in the early 1800s and reached its zenith in the United States. As its name implies—*never* call it "Reformed" Judaism—it rejects many of the cherished beliefs and practices of Orthodoxy, including the authority of the *Halacha*, rabbinic law, and the dietary laws.

In Reform Judaism, worship services include a great deal of English, and the liturgy usually has organ accompaniment. Head coverings and prayer shawls are optional, and women have full rights. They can become Reform rabbis.

Conservative Judaism began in the latter years of the 19th century. It attempts to retain much of Jewish tradition, at the same time recognizing the validity of change and modification in Jewish practice. It accepts *Halacha*, rabbinic law, including the dietary laws.

Worshippers at services in Conservative congregations wear skull caps and, in the case of men, prayer shawls. A considerable amount of English is used in the liturgy to supplement the Hebrew prayers. Organ music is permitted, and women sit with the men.

Recently, Conservative Judaism has approved the ordination of women rabbis.

Your question does not mention it, but there is a fourth denomination in Jewish religion. Reconstructionism is the most recent of the denominations, tracing its origins to the early 1930s in the United States.

Reconstructionism sees Judaism as a civilization and the

synagogue as being potentially the center for local Jewish community life, including the secular aspect.

In structure, Reconstructionist services are similar to those in Conservative congregations, but the Reconstructionist prayer book is closer to today's Reform prayer book.

Rabbinic law is respected as a starting point for changes and modifications ("reconstruction") in Jewish ritual and practice.

Women have full rights in Reconstructionism including that of becoming rabbis.

It is estimated that 85 percent of all American Jews affiliated with synagogues in this country consider themselves as being Reform, Conservative or Reconstructionist, while 15 percent are members of Orthodox congregations.

What is the dogma of Judaism?

Religions typically require their adherents to believe in specific ideas, teachings and interpretations. Judaism does not.

We have neither dogma nor confession of a creed. The nearest we came to those was when the 12th century Jewish philosopher and physician, Moses ben Maimon (Maimonides), formulated his "Thirteen Principles of Faith." These principles, which cover belief in God, resurrection and the coming of the Messiah, are incorporated into the Orthodox Jewish prayer book and in the liturgical hymn, *Yigdal (yig-DAHL),* which is sung in most synagogues.

In no way do Maimonides' Principles constitute Jewish dogma, and a Jew does not have to subscribe to them to be considered a Jew.

You have stated that there are no dogmas in Judaism, but you keep referring to Orthodox law. I'm confused.

Halacha (hah-LAH-khah), the Orthodox legal guideline frequently mentioned in our answers, encompasses Biblical along with the post-Biblical laws, including the Talmud.

Halacha is valid only for those traditional Jews who accept it. There are many Jews who belong to Orthodox synagogues because they enjoy the services and the traditions but who do not adhere, in the main, to the dictates of *Halacha.*

Reform Jews do not follow *Halacha,* and Conservative Judaism is selective in modifying some of the laws.

For a person to consider himself or herself a Jew does not depend on accepting or practicing the guidelines of *Halacha*.

This is quite different from church dogma. If you deny or flaunt such dogma, you run the risk of being expelled or excommunicated.

Judaism provides a huge range of flexibility and room for dissent.

If a Jew converts to another religion, would you still consider him or her to be Jewish?

No! Despite the fact that some Jewish converts to Christianity call themselves "Jews for Jesus" or "Messianic Jews," no branch of Judaism accepts them as Jews.

A number of years ago, a Polish-born Jew who had converted to Christianity during the Holocaust and had joined a Christian religious order settled in a monastery in the State of Israel. "Brother Daniel" claimed automatic Israeli citizenship which is granted Jews who settle in the ancient homeland under the rubric of the Law of the Return.

After much litigation, the Israeli Supreme Court rejected his petition on the basis that a professing Christian cannot be considered a Jew.

Similarly, Jewish young people who affiliate with the Moonies, the International Society for Krsna Consciousness (Hare Krishnas) and esoteric cults and sects are not considered Jews, even if they view themselves as ethnic Jews.

However, any Jew who has converted out of the faith can return to the Jewish fold at any time. Even on his or her deathbed, the expressed desire of a converted Jew to repent and return and to die a Jew and be interred in a Jewish cemetery will be honored.

I have met Spiritualists, Science of Mind followers, Unitarians, Christian Scientists—all of whom have told me that Jews are also members of their churches. Can Jews belong to other religions and still be Jews?

Uh-uh (accompanied by a shaking of the head from side to side, that means a vigorous No)!

Even though some of the churches you mention don't require a statement of adherence to a specific creed, they still are, as a whole, contradictory to the spirit of the Jewish faith.

If you mean by your question, can persons belong to a religion other than Judaism but remain Jews ethnically, the question becomes more sticky. However, the consensus among Jewish authorities as well as lay people would be firmly in the negative.

What is the difference between the Old and New Testaments?

Jews do not speak of the "Old" and "New" Testaments. For Jews, there is only one Bible, the Hebrew Bible, consisting of three parts: the Pentateuch or *Torah (toe-RAH)*, the books of Genesis through Deuteronomy; the Prophets; the Writings, including the Psalms, the book of Proverbs and other sacred writings.

The designation of a "New" Testament is strictly Christian and refers to the anthology of the Gospels, Acts of the Apostles, the Epistles and the Revelation of St. John the Divine.

Christianity accepts the Hebrew Bible as the forerunner of the new dispensation and, accordingly, considers it "old." Judaism disagrees and believes that there is nothing in the Christian Testament which is not already contained in the Hebrew Bible, except for Christological references or teachings which Jews cannot accept.

Do Jews take the Bible literally?

Orthodox Jews believe that the Bible is the revealed word of God. The Pentateuch, the first five books of the Bible (Genesis through Deuteronomy), was revealed to Moses and the ancient Hebrews at Mt. Sinai. The text of these five books was written down by Moses at God's directive, with the exception of the closing verses of Deuteronomy, which record the death of Moses.

Later on, the Hebrew Prophets considered their preachments to be the word of God speaking through them.

Since they believe that the Bible is divinely revealed, traditional Jews would say that what is contained in the Bible supersedes science and human-written history. The Creation story is one example.

Jews who belong to the Reform and Reconstructionist denominations, along with secularist Jews, contend that the Pentateuch is a divinely-*inspired*, rather than revealed, document which was written by many people, not by Moses alone. That means that the Bible is a superb ethical work but not a book of science. For example, Reform and Reconstructionist Jews believe that the Biblical account of Creation should not be viewed as supplanting the scientific theory but as a poetic interpretation of how the world came to be.

Conservative Jews, depending on whether they are "right-wing" or "left-wing," may incline either to the fundamentalist or modernist views of the Bible.

What is "Torah"? I have heard Jewish people speak about it sometimes as if it were the Bible and at other times as if it is more than the Bible. Which is it?

Both. The word *Torah (toe-RAH)* means both "teaching" and "law." When we speak of the Torah specifically—as in "we read from the Torah in the synagogue today"—we refer to the Pentateuch, the first five books of the Hebrew Bible: Genesis, Exodus, Leviticus, Numbers and Deuteronomy.

We also speak of Torah generically; for example, "A Jew should be familiar with Torah." Here, we may be referring to the entire Hebrew Bible plus the Talmud and even, in the broadest sense, to all of Jewish religious writings through the ages.

What is the Talmud? From time to time, I have heard references made to it. Is it different from the Bible?

Indeed, it is different from the Bible. The Talmud is a vast compilation of discussions of Jewish law. It may be compared with a modern court reporter's case records and transcriptions of pleadings before the courts. Majority and minority opinions are reported faithfully and in considerable detail.

Often, the reader must wade through—(it has been called "the sea of the Talmud")—the disputations in ancient Jewish academies and sometimes contradictory decisions in order to discover what is the majority determination.

The first part of the Talmud is the *Mishna (MISH-nah);* the second and larger section is called the *Gemara (geh-MAH-rah).* There are two Talmuds. One is known as the Jerusalem Talmud and was compiled in the Hebrew language around the year 400 C.E. The larger is the Babylonian Talmud, compiled in Babylonia and written in the Aramaic language about a century later.

The Talmud is the basis for *Halacha (hah-LAH-kah),* rabbinic law which is still operative for Orthodox Jews, and, with modifications, for Conservative Jews.

Where does a Jew think God lives?

In condominiums, in hovels, on farms, in high-rises, in factories, in mansions, on Skid Row—wherever people do God's work.

"Where can I find You?" asks a pious Jew in song, and he answers, triumphantly, "And where can I not find you! Eastward—You! Westward—You! Northward—You! Southward—You!"

Do Jews believe God created the world?

Yes, in the same way that all religions presuppose God as Creator. However, for many Jews that does not necessarily mean that the Creation story as it is recounted in the book of Genesis in the Hebrew Bible is accepted as scientifically valid.

Jews have no problem in reconciling scientific theory about the origin of the world with the concept that God is Creator, the Force behind Creation.

It all had to start somewhere!

Do you think God is vengeful and punishing?

No. Adjectives such as "vengeful" and "punishing" describe human traits. Judaism does not believe that God can be defined in anthropomorphic, that is, human terms.

Among contemporary Jews, you may find many who believe that God is a life force, a process, a power that makes for salvation in human beings rather than a supernatural being, given to capriciousness and revenge.

My friend, Dan, claims to be a committed Jew but says he's an atheist. He's kidding about one or the other, isn't he? Or can you be Jewish without believing in God?

Among religiously-committed Jews, the answer would be: No. Belief in the existence of God is basic to being Jewish.

However, there are many people who consider themselves Jews ethnically and culturally, although they are complete non-believers religiously.

Since Judaism permits a wide variation in defining what God is, from a supernatural, personal God to a Process, your friend should be cautious about characterizing himself an atheist, that is, one who denies the existence of God. More likely, he may be an agnostic, one who is skeptical but admits that he doesn't know beyond a doubt that God does not exist.

A number of leading personalities in modern Jewish history could be considered to have been agnostics, among them the founder and first prime minister of the State of Israel, David Ben Gurion, and one of his successors in that office, Golda Maier, as well as the late United States Supreme Court Justice Louis D. Brandeis.

There is in this country a Society for Humanistic Judaism which claims that many notable Jews of the 19th century never prayed, never affiliated with a synagogue and were demonstrably disinterested in God.

I've always thought that Judaism is a religion, but I find that many of the Jewish people with whom I come in contact are not religious. They don't attend synagogue services, and they don't celebrate Jewish holidays. Isn't Judaism a religion? How can these people be considered Jews, if they don't practice their faith?

Judaism is a religion, but it is more than a religion.

The best definition of Judaism is the one formulated in the mid-1930s by Rabbi Mordecai M. Kaplan. Judaism is a *civilization,* Dr. Kaplan argued, and most Jews would agree, because it possesses all the elements that make up a civilization: peoplehood, common history, land of origin, folkways, mores, customs, language (Hebrew, Yiddish, Ladino), literature, art, music and the sense of a common destiny.

There are numbers of Jews who know little about Jewish religion or culture or history but who have a strong sense of ethnicity. They typically are very defensive about real or imagined threats to the Jewish people and are very supportive, financially and politically, of the State of Israel, even though they have no intention of settling there.

While we recognize that there are irreligious Jews, we have to point out that people cannot understand the history of the Jews without appreciating the role of Jewish religion.

That is why Dr. Kaplan added a qualifying adjective to his formulation: Judaism is a *religious* civilization.

And that is why, if you visit Israel on any religious holiday, you will see everyone, even non-religious Jews, celebrating as a sign of national solidarity.

4

The Jewish
View of Jesus

Do Jews believe in Jesus?

Jews do not believe in Jesus, neither as the Messiah nor as the "Son of God."

How can Jews say that Jesus isn't the Messiah?

The Biblical evidence for the coming of the Messiah (or, for most modern Jews, the arrival of the Messianic era) would be the fulfillment of the prophecy about a world where the wolf will dwell with the lamb, the leopard lie down with the kid *(Isaiah 11:6)* and where human beings "shall beat their swords into plowshares and their spears into pruning hooks... neither shall they learn war any more." *(Isaiah 2:4)*

It is impossible for Jews to believe that any of this was fulfilled after the birth and death of Jesus of Nazareth. Instead, in the words of another Hebrew prophet, "they cry peace, peace, when there is no peace." *(Jeremiah 6:14)*

You have quoted from Isaiah to disprove that Jesus was the Messiah. What about Isaiah 53?

The 53rd chapter of Isaiah has for a long, long time been a favorite of missionaries who have sought, in vain, to convince Jews that its verses predict the coming of Jesus as the Messiah.

In his description in this chapter of what has come to be known as the Suffering Servant, the prophet wrote of a person "...wounded because of our sins...by his bruises we were healed...as a lamb who is led to slaughter...they made his grave with the wicked...he bore the sin of many and made intercession for sinners."

This is taken by Christians to be a prophecy of Jesus, his suffering in life and a vicarious atonement through his death on the cross (in Christian doctrine, *agnus dei,* "the lamb of God").

Jewish scholars dispute this interpretation. In this chapter, Isaiah is enigmatic. In the Jewish view, the Suffering Servant may be an individual (perhaps Isaiah, himself, or another one of the prophets of Israel) or the Jewish people as a whole.

The latter view is generally held by Jews; certainly, the history of the Jewish people would match the excerpts from Isaiah quoted above.

In any case, no Jew, scholar or lay person, sees in *Isaiah 53* proof positive, or proof at all, of Jesus being the Messiah.

Jesus referred to Himself as the Son of God and the source of salvation. How does Judaism feel about this?

Since we are all sons and daughters of God, Judaism does not believe that anyone can claim the exclusive title of Son of God and the right to special status that would go with it.

God is the only source of salvation.

Jesus is regarded as the vicarious atonement for the sins of those who accept Him as the Savior. Can Jews believe that Jesus, by His death on the cross, saved us from a terrible fate because of our Original Sin?

The idea that we are born in Original Sin, that we inherit the guilt for the "fall" of Adam and Eve *(Genesis 3:1–8)* is completely alien and unacceptable to Judaism.

Once you deny the concept of Original Sin, there is no need for an "atonement" for the sin; and the need for Jesus as that vicarious atonement becomes moot.

If Jews do not accept Jesus as the Son of God and the Messiah, do you not at least acknowledge that He was a great Jewish Prophet?

Sorry to disappoint you, but the answer has to be in the negative, for two reasons. First, in the Jewish view there is nothing in the teachings ascribed to Jesus that had not already been proclaimed by the Hebrew Prophets long before he appeared on the scene.

The teachings which the Gospels say were those of Jesus often begin with "I say unto you." The Prophets of Israel never claimed that their utterances were their own, but rather that, as Prophets, they were merely communicators of God's word which had come to them. "Thus says the Lord...," for example. *(Isaiah 50:1)*

How can you state that Jesus was not original in the things He taught?

The Golden Rule is found in the sacred writings of nine of the religions of the world, including Judaism.

The Lord's Prayer, the Sermon on the Mount, the Beatitudes, are all taken from verses in the Hebrew Bible.

The defense rests.

If Jews don't believe in Jesus, who or what are "Jews for Jesus"?

This is a cult whose members are, or claim to be, born Jews who now affirm that they have found the fulfillment of their Judaism in accepting Jesus as the Son of God and the Messiah.

The Jewish community—Reform, Conservative, Orthodox, Reconstructionist, Humanist, Secularist—which very often fails to agree on many points—is unanimous in asserting that the philosophy behind the title, "Jews for Jesus," is contradictory and that those born Jews who now profess Jesus are no longer Jews. This applies as well to cults whose members call themselves "Messianic Jews" and "Hebrew Christians."

Was Jesus an observant Jew?

Jesus was raised in the Jewish religion. Joseph and Mary certainly were observant Jews who, among other things, fulfilled the obligation to go to Jerusalem annually to observe Passover. It would follow that Jesus was taught to attend the synagogue and to become familiar with the Hebrew Bible.

The Christian Testament tells us that Jesus attended the synagogue on Saturday, the Jewish Sabbath. As a matter of fact, we read that he launched his public career by arising in the congregation in Nazareth and reading the *haftarah (hahf-tah-RAH),* the selection from the Hebrew Prophet Isaiah for that Sabbath, following the reading from the Pentateuch.

The Gospels assure us that Jesus stressed that he had come to fulfil the Mosaic Law, not to abolish it. At the same time, he asserted his privilege of cancelling or modifying rituals and practices.

It was this tendency to have Jesus act as a one-person decision-maker over Jewish belief, custom and practice that, in part, eventually led to Christianity becoming a religion separate and distinct from its Jewish origins.

Wasn't Jesus called Rabbi?

Probably. However, we must not confuse the more formal status of the rabbi in later centuries and in our own times with the condition of the itinerant preachers who roamed through ancient Judaea, one of whom was apparently Jesus.

What role does Jesus play in Jewish history?

Unfortunately, not a happy one, since so much persecution of Jews was perpetrated by his followers in his name.

Was Moses the Jewish Jesus?

Judaism has gone out of its way to deny divine status to Moses, even to the extent of concealing the place of his death, so that it would not become a shrine. *(Deuteronomy 34:6)*

Moses was the Great Lawgiver, not the Messiah.

My pastor says that the Last Supper was actually a Passover *seder.* If this is so, wasn't Jesus an observant Jew?

The Last Supper most probably was a Passover meal, if not an actual *seder (SAY-dare).* Experts on the Gospels disagree on whether the

Last Supper took place on the first night of Passover, in which case it would have been a *seder,* or on that afternoon. The wine on the "menu" *(Matthew 26:29)* confirms that this was a holiday feast.

Yes, there is every reason to assume that Jesus was an observant Jew, although the writers of the Gospels (written 30 years after his death) tell us that he was dissatisfied with strict observance of Jewish Law.

Did the Jews crucify Jesus?

No. In no way could Jews have crucified him. Since the Romans ruled Judaea, the Jews did not have the kind of power to prescribe or carry out capital punishment of any kind.

Even during an earlier period, when Jews were sovereign in their own commonwealth, crucifixion was never a form of capital punishment. Death on the cross was a Roman "fashion."

According to the Christian Testament, Jesus was tried by the Sanhedrin, which at that time was the supreme Jewish religious tribunal. Aside from the Gospel writers, who obviously were not impartial and who wrote some 30 years after the event, there is no substantiation of this charge.

The teachings of Jesus may have alarmed the Jewish establishment of his time which was responsible for keeping law and order, responsible to the Roman governor of Judaea, Pontius Pilate. It is highly unlikely, however, that the Jewish leaders would have handed over any Jew to the Roman authority.

Jesus was one of countless Jews as well as non-Jews who met their death by crucifixion during Rome's domination of Judaea and the entire ancient world.

According to Christianity, the Resurrection is a guarantee of life after death for everyone who accepts Jesus. What is the Jewish belief?

Relatively few Jews today believe in bodily resurrection. Life after death is understood in a spiritual or allegorical sense.

In an earlier period, the traditional Jewish view of bodily resurrection was associated with the coming of the Messiah. Jews have never accepted Jesus as the Messiah; therefore, they had no need to accept the account of his resurrection in the Gospels.

If you Jews don't believe in Jesus as the Christ and the meaning of His death on the cross, then how on earth do you think you can be saved?

A leading thinker of modern times, the late Rabbi Abraham Joshua Heschel, once observed that a major difference between Christianity and Judaism is that the Christian is preoccupied with how he or she may attain salvation, while the Jew is concerned with how he or she can perform another good deed.

So the concept of salvation in the Christian sense is alien to Judaism. However, Judaism provides routes for deliverance from sin. We try penitence, prayer, charity, worship and deeds of loving-kindness towards all God's creatures.

Do Jews deny that Jesus made a significant contribution to the world?

Most Jews concede that Jesus made a tremendous impact on the Western world through Christianity, which is based on his life and teachings. However, to Jews Jesus is neither the Messiah, nor the Son of God, nor a messenger who has brought Good Tidings.

He plays absolutely no role in Jewish thought, culture or religion.

Why is Christianity called the "daughter of Judaism" when they are so different?

Judaism and Christianity are different, but they have more in common with each other than with the religions of the East.

Many years ago, a distinguished, liberal Christian clergyperson delivered a sermon to his congregation in The Community Church of New York City entitled "Christianity's Debt to Judaism." In it, Dr. John Haynes Holmes indicated some of the close relationships between Christianity and Judaism which have led people to describe Christianity as the daughter of Judaism:

Mary and Joseph were Jews.

Their child, Jesus, was born a Jew.

Jesus was reared and trained in the Jewish faith.

The Hebrew Bible, which comprises some three-fourths of the Christian Bible, is "Jewish through and through; and whenever Christians use it they should remember that they are turning to Jewish sources for instruction and inspiration."

Every word of the Christian Testament, from the first chapter of Matthew to the last chapter of Revelation, was written by Jews.

The institution and liturgy of the church was modeled on the synagogue.

The Christian Sabbath is based on the Jewish Sabbath, although Christianity changed the Sabbath day to Sunday.

From Judaism came such key teachings in Christianity as the Golden Rule, the Lord's Prayer, the Beatitudes, the Sermon on the Mount, as well as the closing verses of the 12th chapter of Paul's Epistle to the Romans.

Indeed, Christianity is appropriately characterized as the daughter of Judaism. A daughter—or son—may differ markedly from the parents and yet may bear many similarities.

5

Marriage Between Jews and People Who Aren't

I am in love with a wonderful Jewish man, who would like to marry me. However, he insists that I convert to Judaism before our marriage, in order to keep peace in his family. I do not feel that this is a good reason for me to convert, but I love and respect Steve; and I don't want to lose him. Any advice?

Even if you should be willing, conversion to Judaism just to "keep peace" in Steve's family is neither honest nor would it be acceptable, according to Jewish practice.

While three out of every 10 non-Jewish spouses in today's inter-marriages convert to Judaism, the Jewish view is that conversion must never be a consequence of duress or "for appearances." The decision to convert has to grow out of the commitment and sincere desire of the individual to embrace Judaism whole-heartedly after studying and understanding the religion and the civilization of the Jewish people.

Unfortunately, but realistically, this is one of the first challenges a couple contemplating a mixed marriage is forced to confront.

Honest exploration and communication of feelings and attitudes can be genuine peacekeepers in relationships. Stick with them.

Charades for public display usually lead to bottled-up, accumulated resentment.

How do you feel about Jewish parents who would disown their son, because he married an Episcopalian woman? Our daughter, Marge, married Adam in a civil ceremony three years ago. His parents refused to attend the wedding and have since rejected all his attempts at communication.

We suspect that the relationship between Adam and his parents left something to be desired long before he met your daughter.

A loving tie between parents and a child cannot and should not be broken, even because of a marriage which might not be to the parents' liking.

Centuries ago, when a marriage between a Jew and a non-Jew almost always meant that the Jewish person converted to the religion of the non-Jew and joined the church, the Jewish parents would disown the child and never speak to him or her again, treating their child as having died.

However, times and circumstances have changed. Understanding and communication are required, even under trying conditions, to keep a sense of love and compassion in a family.

I had a real shocker the other day. We were at the home of a Jewish couple with whom we've been close for years. Our 9-year-old son and their 8-year-old daughter were playing ball with Jonathan, their dog, when I said something to the effect of "Wouldn't it be something, if Jim and Susie got married some day." "Oh, that won't happen, because Jim isn't Jewish," blurted out my friend. I couldn't believe it. My husband and I got the impression that, suddenly, our son wouldn't be good enough for their daughter.

The reluctance of your Jewish friends to accept a union between their daughter and your son is not a question of "good enough." It springs, rather, from an assortment of feelings, some of them gut reactions, others very rational.

Consider the almost instinctual and understandable desire of a tiny minority—Jewish, in this instance—to maintain its group identity and keep from being swallowed up in the non-Jewish majority and disappearing from the scene of history. The will to live, to survive, expresses itself.

Religious, cultural and ethnic differences tend to become more emphasized as people grow older. Young people may maintain that religion and ethnicity mean little or nothing to them; but, very often, the passage of time and the aging process accentuates rather than diminishes the differences.

As men and women mature, observe their once-strapping parents deteriorate and pass away, and realize that their own youthful dreams have been only partially fulfilled, if at all, they typically reach back and try to grab on to the traditions of childhood for solace and security.

These include religious, cultural and ethnic traditions, replete with holiday celebrations and often regular synagogue and church-going.

Contributing the differences of religion, culture and ethnicity to the tensions and hazards operative in modern marriage is a risky undertaking.

The coming of children into a mixed marriage exacerbates the problem. Young parents who, up to that point, had considered themselves unconcerned with religious differences suddenly find each other opinionated when the first child arrives, often goaded by the grandparents, to be sure.

Choices such as baptism/christening vs. Jewish ritual circumcision, Christmas tree vs. Hanukkah menorah, type of Sunday school, First Communion vs. Bar/Bat Mitzvah often have to be made and become sources of tension and abrasion.

An added factor is the escalated divorce rate in this country. The religious upbringing of the children of such broken unions may depend on the preference of the parent who is granted custody by the court.

With the increasing number of marriages between Jews and non-Jews in the United States (between 40 and 50 percent), you can probably come up with at least one instance of a mixed marriage which appears to be working out just fine. Your Jewish friends, however, are concerned less with statistics than with the prospect of their daughter and their future grandchildren being lost to Judaism.

All this does not mean that your Jewish friends do not like you or your husband or value your friendship. Why don't you dialogue with them, "touch bases" on the matter, instead of permitting it to continue on the level of hints and inferences?

Our son, Rich, is seriously involved with a Jewish girl. We are very concerned about the relationship, even though we are very fond of Sandy. Rich says we are anti-Semitic. That is untrue, but we want to be able to share our heritage and holidays with our son and grandchildren. How can we convince Rich and Sandy that we are not anti-Semites?

It is entirely possible that Rich is using the accusation of anti-Semitism to manipulate both of you into approving of a marriage which you find difficult to accept for the same reason Jewish parents, confronted with the same type of situation, panic: the fear of change in family lifestyle and continuity.

On the other hand, does Rich have some evidence, based on the values you taught him in his earlier years, to believe that you harbor feelings of resentment, or whatever, against Jews?

As in the instance of Jewish parents in the same situation, you have to walk a very careful path between not trying to run your adult son's life, while at the same time calmly and logically making your position clear.

In any case, you should not, and must not, confuse the issue here with your feelings for Sandy, of whom you say you are very fond. Keep both Rich and Sandy aware of your warm feelings for her, at the same time being forthright about your concerns.

Then, let nature take its course. It will, anyhow.

Our pastor is perfectly agreeable to having a rabbi join him in officiating at the church wedding of our daughter, Melissa, to Dan, her Jewish fiance. Dan's family rabbi says no. What do you think?

Rabbis of all four Jewish denominations, Orthodox, Reform, Conservative and Reconstructionist, are on record as being opposed to officiating at mixed marriages, those involving a Jew and a non-Jew. (Remember, if the non-Jewish person converts, he or she is Jewish.)

Some Reform rabbis will perform mixed marriages. Very few of them, however, would co-officiate with a Christian minister. It is even rarer to find a rabbi who would co-officiate with a Christian minister at a wedding in a church.

Until recent years, Protestant and, especially, Roman Catholic clergy were adamantly opposed to officiating at weddings between members of their faiths and persons of a different religion. Their opposition, however, has been greatly muted, leaving rabbis in a somewhat isolated position.

Rabbis feel that requests for their presence at the nuptials is part of a charade, intended solely to placate the parents or grandparents of the Jewish bride or bridegroom. There would seem to be no other logical explanation, since the non-Jewish member of the bridal pair has clearly indicated objection to converting to the Jewish faith.

Jewish marriage vows are exchanged "according to the Law of Moses and of Israel." The intrinsic character of a mixed marriage nullifies the validity of such vows.

Rabbis do not believe their ordination sanctions playing a role in the liquidation of the integrity of the Jewish faith or the numbers of the Jewish people.

6

What Do You Mean,
You Want to
Become a Jew?

Do Jews actively look for converts?

If you are under the impression that Judaism isn't keen about accepting converts...not so! As far back as the story of Ruth in the Hebrew Bible, Judaism has welcomed the sincere convert who, like Ruth, makes the voluntary commitment that "Your people shall be my people and your God my God." *(Ruth 1:16)*

However, for many, many centuries Jews were a harrassed minority. From the time that Christianity became the religion of the Roman Empire and, subsequently, when Islam dominated the world scene, Jews were forbidden either to look for converts or even to accept them.

These days, any reluctance rabbis might have in encouraging conversion to Judaism has to do with the applicant's intent and maturity. If the reasons offered by the prospective convert appear immature or frivolous, such as "I'm dating a Jewish girl" or "I really couldn't care less; I'm doing it to please my fiance's parents," most rabbis will show little enthusiasm.

In fact, rabbis will seriously attempt on three occasions to discourage the prospective proselyte, in an attempt to make sure that only the most committed go through with the conversion.

Conversion to Judaism is not the single act of affirmation of a creed, as in Christianity, but becoming a member of a minority which has a long history of being victimized, discriminated against and subjected to bodily harm. It is difficult for a person born and reared in a majority Christian culture to accept the history of the Jews as his or her personal history and to identify with Jewish aspirations and anxieties.

In our church, we support a worldwide mission outreach program. Do synagogues support Jewish missionary efforts?

No. While converts to Judaism are accepted and welcomed, there is no organized Jewish missionary activity.

Can't I become Jewish just by joining a synagogue?

No, because you can't join a synagogue in the first place unless you are Jewish!

You, or anyone, can attend worship services at any synagogue without question. But the moment you ask to join, that is, apply for formal membership in the synagogue, you will be accepted only if you are a Jew, by birth or conversion.

Putting it another way, synagogue membership does not automatically confer Jewish status upon the person. First you become formally Jewish; then you join the congregation.

How would I go about converting to Judaism?

Your initial step is as near as your telephone. Call a rabbi of any one of the Jewish denominations: Reform, Conservative, Reconstructionist, Orthodox, and set up an appointment to sit down with him or her. You don't have to make a commitment in advance.

Preparation for conversion involves:

• Study over a period of several months either privately with a rabbi or in one of the classes which are available in larger cities. You would read about basic Judaism and Jewish history, listen to lectures and take part in discussions about the beliefs and practices of Judaism and how they differ from Christianity and other religions, as well as visit local synagogues to become familiar with what Jewish religious services are like.

• In Orthodox and Conservative Judaism, the course of study is followed by a ceremony of immersion in water called a *MIHK-vah*—

don't call it "baptism"—and, for a man, ritual circumcision (a token procedure if the man is already circumcised). Reform rabbis may or may not require immersion and/or circumcision.

• Now you are ready for the formal conversion ceremony before three witnesses, usually rabbis, during which you are asked formally to renounce your previous religious beliefs and to recite the *Shema (sheh-MAH),* the Hebrew statement of belief in One God. *(Deuteronomy 6:4).*

• You will be given a Hebrew name, which will be in addition to your English name. You will be known as "the son (or daughter) of Abraham our father and Sara our mother," thereby linking your conversion with the beginnings of Jewish history.

The conversion ceremony may take place in the study of one of the participating rabbis or on the pulpit of a synagogue. You will be presented with a conversion certificate.

I am an uncircumcised non-Jew who would like to become Jewish. The thought of being circumcised petrifies me. What can I do?

We can certainly understand your concern and anxiety. Perhaps some of the following explanation may help clarify the situation and, hopefully, reduce your fears.

As you may know, there is a body of medical wisdom, by no means unanimous, which recommends circumcision as a hygienically beneficial procedure.

Circumcision, even for an adult male, is a simple surgical procedure which can certainly be tolerated with the aid of anesthesia. It can be performed by a *mohel (MO-hell),* a Jewish ritual circumciser, or by a Jewish M.D.

Orthodox and Conservative Judaism require circumcision as a precondition for the final conversion of a man who has not previously been circumcised. If he has, a token drop of blood is acceptable.

Reform rabbis frequently bypass the requirement of circumcision. If your anxieties over having to undergo circumcision persist, pursue your conversion plans under the direction of a Reform rabbi.

7

Celebrating
Jewish Holidays

**It seems to me that my Jewish neighbor is always observing
her religious holidays. These special days seem to be tripping
over each other, especially in the early Fall. How come?**

It's not quite that congested, although our holidays do appear to be
bunched up during September and October.

First, there is *Rosh Hashanah (rosh hah-shah-NAH)*, the New
Year which commemorates Creation, "the birthday of the world."
Conservative and Orthodox Jews observe it for two days, Reform
Jews for one day. Rosh Hashanah can occur anywhere from early
September to early October, since the Hebrew calendar differs from
the secular calendar.

Ten days later comes *Yom Kippur (yome kih-POOR)*, the Day of
Atonement, the most solemn day in our religious calendar, when
Jews search their inmost selves and try to atone for their defects
and sins.

Five days after Yom Kippur, we celebrate *Sukkot (soo-KOTE)*, the
Festival of Booths, which reminds Jews of the time when their Hebrew ancestors, traveling from Egypt to the Promised Land, would
sleep in frail lean-tos each night of their journey. Sukkot is also a
harvest festival.

Eight days later, Sukkot ends, and *Simhat Torah (sim-KHAHT
toe-RAH)* begins. This is when we Rejoice Over the Torah. Jews read

a section of the Pentateuch every week at Sabbath services and come full circle in the annual cycle on Simhat Torah.

We have a two-month breather until *Hanukkah (KHAH-noo-kah)*, the Festival of Lights and Dedication. Hanukkah is observed for eight days towards the end of November or some time in December and recalls the first successful struggle for religious freedom.

Another gap, this time of three months, until *Purim (POO-reem)*, the Feast of Lots, a carnival-like holiday which recalls the escape of the Jews of ancient Persia from annihilation.

One month after Purim, usually in April, we celebrate the eight-day Freedom Festival of Passover, *Pesach (PEH-sahkh)* in Hebrew. We tell the story of how Moses led the Hebrew slaves out of Egypt.

Shavuot (shah-voo-OTE), the early summer harvest festival, is a memorial of the giving of the Ten Commandments by God on Mount Sinai to Moses and the Jewish people. It is called the Feast of Weeks, because it occurs seven weeks after Passover.

All is quiet until the holiday cycle begins again with Rosh Hashanah.

Here's a bonus! There are some less important occasions which many Jews you know may not observe.

Hamisha Asar B'Shvat (khah-mee-SHAH ah-SAHR bish-VAHT)— also known as *Tu B'Shvat (too bish-VAHT)*, the 15th day of the Hebrew month of Shvat, occurs in January and is called Jewish Arbor Day or the "New Year of the Trees."

Lag B'omer (lahg beh-OH-mehr) in May is the 33rd day following the second day of Passover and is called "the scholars' festival."

Tisha B'Av (tee-SHAH beh-AHV), the ninth day of the month of Av, is a day for fasting, because it recalls tragic events in Jewish history, such as the destruction of the First and Second Temples in Jerusalem.

Few Jews, even those who claim not to be religious, will go to work or school on the Jewish New Year and Day of Atonement. Observant Jews will refrain from work on the opening and closing days of the festivals of Sukkot, Passover and Shavuot.

People don't have to skip work or school on Hanukkah and Purim.

Since World War II, two additional observances have been added to the Jewish calendar. *Yom Hashoa (yome hah-SHOW-ah)* means Holocaust Day and is a memorial to the six million Jews who were killed by the Nazis under Hitler. It is observed in April or May, fluctuating with the Jewish calendar.

Eight days later, Israel Independence Day, known in Hebrew as

Yome Hah-ahts-mah-OOT, celebrates the event in 1948 when the Jews of Israel proclaimed that country a sovereign state.

How do you arrive at the figure for the Jewish New Year? For example, if a year is numbered 5746, when was the year 1?

In the 12th century, Jewish scholars, working from computations of happenings recorded in the Bible, came to the conclusion that the Year 1, the year Creation took place, was 3761 Before the Common Era.

Judaism does not claim that this reckoning has any relationship to the scientific estimate that the world is billions of years old.

After all, it's easier to put 5746 on a Jewish New Year greeting card than it would be to print 5,746,000,000!

Why isn't the Jewish New Year on January 1?

The origin of the Jewish religious New Year is to be found in the Bible, which refers to the first day of the month of *Tishri (TIHSH-ree)* as "a sacred occasion commemorated with loud blasts" of the horn. *(Leviticus 23:24; Numbers 29:1)*

Since the Jewish month of *Tishri* usually falls in September, and since the first day of *Tishri* is *Rosh Hashanah (rosh hah-shah-NAH),* the Jewish New Year cannot occur on January 1.

How can I wish a special Jewish friend a Happy Jewish New Year? Are gifts appropriate?

Just letting your friend know that you are aware that it is his or her New Year will mean a lot. Since Jews are a minority in the United States, even the important days of *Rosh Hashanah (rosh hah-shah-NAH)* get "lost in the shuffle."

A telephone call will do it. A greeting card would be charming. If your friend is really that "special," you might want to send flowers, a plant, wine or a basket of fruit.

Many Jews still follow a time-honored and lovely custom of holding "open house" on *Rosh Hashanah* afternoon. Your visit would be the nicest way of all of saying Happy New Year!

During the past year, I've become friendly with a Jewish woman who teaches at the same college as I do. Linda and I get together over lunch every Monday, Wednesday and Friday to discuss our husbands, our students and, once in a while, the dean—not necessarily in that order. We have visited each other's homes and even exchanged small birthday gifts. I thought we were building a solid friendship...until Linda blew up at me for not wishing her a Happy Jewish New Year. I didn't know I was supposed to; how could I have known?

Your bewilderment is certainly understandable. You're angry that Linda blamed you for not doing something she wanted done, something that you had no idea she wanted.

This lack of communication between you and Linda frequently exists between Jews and friends who are not.

It's terrific when we Jews hear "Happy New Year" around *Rosh Hashanah (rosh hah-shah-NAH)* and *Yom Kippur (yome kih-POOR)* from our friends who are not Jewish. The greeting makes us feel warm and cozy and totally accepted for who we are.

Come September, TV stations, especially in the larger cities, flash Happy New Year wishes to the Jewish community, and newspapers carry stories about local observances.

Card and gift stores display Jewish New Year cards. And most calendars highlight the Jewish High Holy Days.

So, wish us "Happy New Year"...and don't be surprised if we wish the same to you!

Why do Jewish holidays always begin at night?

Unlike the Gregorian calendar which we use in the Western world, the Jewish calendar is a lunar-solar one and is greatly influenced by the cycle of the moon. For example, the appearance of a new moon signals the beginning of a new month in the Jewish calendar.

Similarly, the appearance of the moon in the sky is regarded as the beginning of a new day according to our calendar.

Keep in mind that in the Biblical account of each day of Creation, the description concludes with the verse, "And there was evening and there was morning..." *(Genesis 1:5, 8, 13, 19, 23, 31)*

Since each day begins at sunset, holidays begin and end with the appearance of the moon and stars.

Why do Jewish holidays fall on different dates every year? One year, a Jewish fellow in our office took off a day at the end of September to observe your New Year. The next year, he took a day off in the middle of September.

As we have just explained, the Jewish calendar is governed by the course of the moon, so there is a discrepancy between the dates of that calendar and those of the Gregorian calendar which we and you use and which is governed by the cycle of the sun. Therefore, the dates on which Jewish holidays fall vary from year to year in the Gregorian calendar.

At the same time, the lunar months of the Jewish calendar must not get too far away from the seasons of the year. Festivals such as Passover, Shavuot and Sukkot, for example, must always be celebrated, respectively, in the Spring, Summer and Fall.

To reconcile both calendars, the Jewish lunar calendar features a built-in, self-adjusting device which adds a leap year month, not just a leap year day. In this way, the Jewish calendar corrects itself and does not get too far out of sync.

Is Hanukkah the most important Jewish holiday?

Considering all the publicity that the eight-day Festival of *Hanukkah (KHAH-noo-kah)* receives these days, it may come as a surprise to learn that it is a minor holiday in the Jewish religious calendar. Observant Jews are not required to skip work or school on Hanukkah, and there are no special synagogue services, apart from added readings in the liturgy.

Hanukkah is a very meaningful holiday, because it commemorates the first struggle in recorded history for religious freedom, the successful campaign waged in Judaea under the leadership of the Maccabees against the Greco-Syrian empire in 165 B.C.E.

Jewish tradition assigned Hanukkah a minor role among the holidays, because it commemorates a military victory, even though the "military" aspect was a successful rebellion against tyranny and not playing "lead soldiers."

The reason that Hanukkah is often and mistakenly assumed to be more important than it is in the list of Jewish holidays is that it coincides with the Christmas season. In an effort to compensate for the fact that Jews do not observe the birth of Jesus, many Jews have "hyped up" Hanukkah. This explains why giving gifts, especially to children, has become such a big thing on Hanukkah. The masters of the marketplace know a good thing when they see it; so Hanukkah, like Christmas, has become highly commercialized.

Should I give my Jewish boyfriend eight Hanukkah gifts, one for each night of the holiday?

No. That is a practice intended for children, to heighten their anticipation and to counter the gift-giving frenzy that characterizes the Christmas season.

One nice gift of some substance would be sufficient. Remember, in homes where gifts are given to the kids each night of Hanukkah, the presents on the first seven nights are usually inexpensive, trivial ones, with the big gift saved for the eighth and final night of the holiday.

If the two of you decide that it would be fun to exchange small gifts for eight nights, go for it. A mutual understanding is what's important here.

I am engaged to a Jewish man. Michael's parents have invited me to their Passover *seder*. About two dozen relatives whom I have never met will be there. Never having attended a *seder* before and knowing nothing about the ritual, I'm concerned that I will embarrass Michael. Would I be better off declining the invitation?

Definitely not! You would be doing a disservice to yourself as well as to Michael and his family by absenting yourself.

The *seder (SAY-dare)* banquet on Passover is probably the warmest family occasion in the Jewish calendar. The narration of the freedom story from the *Haggada (hah-GAH-dah)* has a message for all people, no matter their creed, color, race or national origin.

Have Michael show you ahead of time a copy of the *Haggada* which the family will be using (there is a wide variety) and ask him to explain the highlights of the Passover narrative and what to expect during the evening.

When you get to the *seder,* relax. Ask all the questions you like. The more questions the children and adults ask at a *seder,* the more successful it is.

We hope that Michael's family will do full justice to the *seder* spirit and not just make a big meal of it.

In either event: Enjoy! Enjoy!

I have been invited to attend a Passover Seder. I'd like to bring a gift. Any suggestions?

Since Passover is a Spring festival, we recommend gifts that symbolize that season of the year: a bunch of daisies, carnations or roses. A plant. How about full-blooming African violets, or a small Ficus Benjamina, or a friendly, cascading Creeping Charlie?

Or, stuff a basket with apples, oranges and bananas. Or, fill a cache pot with nuts in their shells—and add a nutcracker.

If you should decide to give wine, candies or baked goods, remember that they must bear a "Kosher for Passover" imprimatur from a rabbinical authority who is specifically named. Hard liquor, mixed drinks—anything made from grain alcohol—is not permitted for consumption on Passover.

Why don't Jews eat bread on Passover?

In describing the hasty departure of the Israelite slaves from Egypt, the Bible *(Exodus 12:39)* tells us that they baked "unleavened cakes," since they didn't have time to let the dough rise in the usual manner.

To recall that event, most Jews eat unleavened bread, *matza (MAH-tsah),* instead of leavened bread during the eight days of Passover.

8

Christmas and Easter: Should We or Shouldn't We?

Why do Jews get so upset when a creche is displayed in public places during the Christmas season?

The overwhelming majority of American Jews are staunch advocates of the Constitutional guarantees for the separation of church and state. Jewish history is, in part, a record of persecution and inequality suffered in countries where there was a state religion, usually Christianity.

The use of governmental property—local, state or federal—to display the symbols of *any* religion, is viewed by most Jews with distrust. When a citizen walks into a city hall, a seat of county government, a state legislature or our national Capitol, he or she should feel that the edifice and the land on which it is built belongs to him or her and to all citizens.

If, during the Christmas season, that governmental property houses a Nativity scene portraying the infant Jesus, Mary and Joseph and the Three Kings, the non-Christian visitor feels that he/she is suddenly an outsider, a non-belonger.

Adding a *menorah (meh-NO-rah)*, a *Hanukkah (KHAH-noo-kah)* candelabrum, is equally wrong.

The opposition, then, is not to displaying the creche in public places but on tax-supported municipal, state or federal property.

Traditionally, our country's courts have buttressed the wall of separation between church and state. However, in major cases in 1983 and 1984, a U.S. Supreme Court decision upheld a Nativity display paid for by municipal tax funds in Pawtucket, Rhode Island. This decision alarmed the Jewish community which, just two years before, had hailed a federal court injunction halting the city of Redondo Beach, California, from sponsoring and paying for Easter sunrise services.

Should I send my Jewish friends Christmas cards or wish them a Merry Christmas?

No, to both parts of your query. Christmas is not a Jewish event. An innocuous "Seasons Greetings" might be acceptable, since it could refer to *Hanukkah (KHAH-noo-kah)* and to the New Year on January 1.

Shall I give my Jewish friends gifts at Hanukkah or Christmas?

Hanukkah (KHAH-noo-kah) is the time for gift-giving to Jews; Christmas is the season for gifts to Christians.

You give a birthday gift to someone on his or her birthday, not on yours!

May I invite Jewish friends to my Christmas party?

You certainly may. One of the bonuses of living in a multi-cultural, multi-ethnic, multi-religious society is that members of one cultural, ethnic or religious group may be invited to enjoy the festivities of another's holidays without being obligated to practice the other culture or religion.

So, in turn, you may expect to be invited to Hanukkah parties, a Passover *seder (SAY-dare)*, Bar/Bat Mitzvahs and other events in the lives of your Jewish friends.

Is Hanukkah the Jewish Christmas?

Negative! This is a common misconception. *Hanukkah (KHAH-noo-kah)* and Christmas have nothing whatsoever to do with one another, except for the fact that they both occur around the season of the Winter solstice.

While Christmas commemorates the birth of the Christian Savior, Hanukkah recalls the first successful battle for religious freedom by the Judaeans against the Greco-Syrian empire in 165 B.C.E.

Interestingly, the Catholic church now urges its adherents to take recognition of the eight-day Jewish festival of Hanukkah on the premise that had the Jews not been triumphant in their struggle to preserve the integrity of their faith in ancient days, Christianity could not have come into existence.

All the homeowners on our block put up elaborate Christmas displays. People come from miles away to look at the rooftop Santas, the elegant Nativity displays on the lawns and the colorful lighting effects. The first Jewish family has now moved on our block. Can we ask them to keep the block tradition by putting up decorations?

It would not be appropriate for a Jewish family, which would otherwise not accept Christmas and its theme of the Nativity, to decorate the exterior of their house with Christmas-type lights and ornaments.

It *would* be in order and highly desirable that they display a large *menorah (meh-NO-rah)*, the nine-branched Hanukkah candelabrum, on their front lawn, as well as display a candle-lit or electric *menorah* in the front window for all to see.

The kindling of one additional light on each of the eight nights of the Hanukkah festival would make a dramatic and colorful addition to the block's festive appearance.

One caution: the Hanukkah decorations belong to the actual eight days of that festival and should not be displayed to coincide with Christmas, unless these two holidays happen to come together in December, as they frequently do.

Our Jewish neighbors trim a Christmas tree and festoon their home with lights and holly wreaths each year. When I happened to mention this to a Jewish co-worker, she became outraged. My neighbors are nice, generous people. It bothers me that my colleague at work made negative comments about them. Why did she have to do this?

It really is unfair, if not downright hypocritical, for someone to take the frills of Christmas and make them a part of their own lifestyle without also accepting the message of Christmas.

For Jewish people, who do not celebrate the birth of the Messiah in a manger in Bethlehem, to accept the external trappings of Christmas, such as the tree, is to display an intellectual dishonesty which is an insult to professing Christians.

It is also an insult to the overwhelming numbers of Jews who are comfortable in their commitment to their faith and do not need to poach on other religions to make their homes more beautiful or their lives happier.

Is Passover the Jewish Easter?

Passover is the Festival of Freedom, during which Jews recall the Exodus from slavery in Egypt by the ancient Israelites and rededicate themselves to the ideal of freedom for all in today's world.

Easter commemorates the Resurrection of Jesus, according to Christian theology.

Obviously, the events have nothing to do with one another. However, both are Spring festivals. Easter occurs at the same season as Passover, because the events that Easter recalls took place during the Passover season. For example, Jesus entered Jerusalem on what has come to be known as Palm Sunday to observe the Jewish Passover; and the Last Supper very likely was a Passover banquet.

Passover is no more the "Jewish Easter" than *Hanukkah (KHAH-noo-kah)* is the "Jewish Christmas."

Do you observe Lent?

Like Easter, Lent focuses on the life and personality of Jesus, leading up to the Passion and Crucifixion. This period of fasting and penitence for Christians, beginning with Ash Wednesday, plays no part whatsoever in Judaism.

I am in a quandry. I will be giving an Easter brunch after church services. Our church holds beautiful services with an outstanding choir. I would like to invite Jewish friends to the brunch and also to the service which will precede it. My husband says that it would be wrong to invite Jewish people to the service, that they might think I was trying to convert them, or they might come in order not to offend me and then feel uncomfortable. I disagree. Everyone else at the brunch will have attended the service, and I don't want these friends to feel that they weren't included, because they are Jewish. Who is right?

Your husband's reasoning is logical, but you win! Your Jewish friends should be given the option and told that they are more than welcome to attend the service with the other brunch guests, but that you and your husband will understand, and certainly not be insulted, if they choose to come to the brunch only.

In short, give your friends the choice and let them decide. Your husband is overly sensitive on one point, though: no one will think you are trying to convert him or her.

Caution: If Easter and Passover coincide, there are certain foods observant Jews will not be able to eat because of Passover dietary restrictions. Check with them.

9

Where Jews Pray, Study and Get Together

Why don't you call your church a church?

"Church," which comes from the Greek and means "the Lord's house," has been the name for a Christian house of worship ever since it appeared in the Christian Testament in a statement by Jesus. *(Matthew 16:18)*

"Synagogue" is also derived from the Greek and means "assembly." As such, it is identical to one of the three Hebrew phrases by which Jews designate their religious center and which means "house of assembly." The other two descriptions are "house of study" and "house of prayer."

"Church" has come to have an exclusively Christian connotation. Neither Jew, Muslim, Shintoist nor followers of other faiths would call their religious centers churches. Throughout history, the word synagogue has come to apply solely to Jewish places of worship.

Some Jewish people I know go to "temple." Others go to "synagogue." What's the difference?

There is no difference. At one period in the early years of Reform Judaism, its leaders took to calling their synagogues "temples" to emphasize the distinction from what they saw as the old-fashioned Orthodox synagogues.

In our times, however, the distinction is meaningless.

What's inside a synagogue?

A synagogue has three functions: house of prayer, schoolhouse for young and old, and a community center.

Let's talk about the latter two functions first. As an educational facility for teaching children, teen-agers and adults, it will have classrooms and a library.

As a community center, a synagogue will have a public hall and kitchen for meetings and social gatherings.

The function of worship takes place in the sanctuary. The main body of the sanctuary is similar to that of a church. You will find seats or pews, a choir loft and (except in Orthodox synagogues) an organ.

The focal point of the synagogue is the pulpit. Located in front of the sanctuary, it has lecterns for the rabbi, who usually conducts the service, and for the cantor, who is in charge of the musical liturgy.

In the center rear of the pulpit is the Holy Ark, which contains the *Torah* Scrolls, hand-printed on parchment, covered with decorative mantles and containing the text of the Pentateuch. Each scroll may have silver ornaments: a breastplate, crown, bells. Depending on how well-to-do a synagogue is, it may have many *Torah* Scrolls.

A curtain covers the Ark, and an Eternal Light, usually electric, burns constantly above the Ark.

What's in a *Torah* Scroll?

A *Torah* Scroll contains the complete text of the Pentateuch, the first five books of the Hebrew Bible, sometimes called the Five Books of Moses: Genesis, Exodus, Leviticus, Numbers and Deuteronomy.

The Hebrew text is painstakingly hand-lettered in a kind of calligraphy by a scribe who specializes in this type of religious artistry.

A particular synagogue may have a number of *Torah* Scrolls, depending upon its affluence.

What goes on in a synagogue during a service?

Praying, singing and sermonizing.

The service is usually conducted by a rabbi, while a cantor is responsible for the musical portion of the liturgy, sometimes together with a choir.

The order of the service follows the prayer book which each worshipper has. The service is a mixture of Hebrew and English: more Hebrew than English in an Orthodox service, more of a balance between the two in Reform and Conservative services.

Each of the denominations mentioned above, as well as the Reconstructionist, has its own prayer book; but all contain readings from the Biblical book of Psalms and other parts of the Hebrew Bible together with prayers and hymns that were written specifically for worship.

Services on Jewish Sabbaths (Friday evenings and Saturday mornings) and holidays will have a segment during which the *Torah* Scrolls are taken from the Holy Ark in procession, and portions are read from the Pentateuch as a Scripture lesson. (It is during this period that a *Bar* or *Bat Mitzvah* would take place.)

The rabbi usually delivers a sermon or homily, which is followed by a choir anthem or cantorial solo. The president or another officer of the congregation will make the announcements of the week.

The service concludes with a prayer for the coming of God's Kingdom upon earth, a memorial prayer for the departed, and a closing hymn.

Following the Sabbath Eve service on Friday night, a collation takes place. It is called an *Oneg Shabbat (OH-nehg shah-BAHT)*, a "Sabbath delight," from *Isaiah 58:13*. Here, everyone socializes while munching on refreshments.

In addition to worship services on Friday evenings, Saturday mornings and holidays, all Orthodox and most Conservative synagogues hold two services each weekday and on Sundays and a Saturday sundown service. These devotions are conducted in the early morning and at sunset.

Do Jews kneel and put the palms of their hands together when they pray?

This typical posture of Christian prayer plays no part in Jewish worship, although the Hebrew Bible does refer to kneeling. *(First Kings 8:54* and *Ezra 9:6)*

There is some bending of the knee by the Jewish worshipper, but no actual kneeling. It occurs at the conclusion of the Jewish liturgy, during the *Alenu (ah-LAY-noo)* prayer for the establishment of God's kingdom. We read, "We bow the head and bend the knee and offer worship and allegiance to the Supreme Sovereign, the Holy One..." Nevertheless, no actual genuflection takes place.

Cantors in Orthodox and Conservative synagogues do kneel and prostrate themselves before the Holy Ark during *Yom Kippur (yome kih-POOR)*, Day of Atonement, rites, emulating the ritual of the High Priests in the Temple in Jerusalem thousands of years ago.

The placing together of the palms of one's hands in prayerful supplication is alien to Jewish worshippers.

I invited a Jewish couple to a Friday night party at my home. They told me they couldn't accept, because they would be attending Sabbath services. What services? Aren't Sabbath services held on Sundays?

The Jewish Sabbath is on the seventh day of the week, because the Bible refers to God as having done the work of creation in six days and having rested on the seventh. *(Exodus 20:8–11)*

The seventh day is Saturday. Since all Jewish days begin at sundown of the previous day, Jewish Sabbath services are held on Friday evenings and Saturday mornings.

The Christian Testament indicates that Jesus, "as his custom was," went into the synagogue on the Jewish Sabbath to worship, teach and heal. *(Luke 4:16)*

Early Christians, many of whom had been Jews, continued to observe the Sabbath on the seventh day. Gradually, however, the observance of the Sabbath was moved to the first day of the week in commemoration of the Resurrection *(Mark 16 ff.)* and the time for breaking bread *(Acts 20:7* and *First Corinthians 16:1 ff.)* for gathering offerings for the poor.

By the way, Seventh Day Adventists, who are Christians, of course, as well as members of the Worldwide Church of God, observe Saturday as their Sabbath. That's why the former are called "Seventh Day" Adventists.

Would I be welcome at a service in a synagogue, even though I am not Jewish?

Absolutely, and you don't have to announce your coming in advance. All synagogues have services on the Sabbath (Friday evenings and Saturday mornings) as well as on the festivals of Passover, *Shavuot (shah-voo-OTE)* and *Sukkot (soo-KOTE)*.

The only time you would have to make advance arrangements with the synagogue office is to attend services on the Jewish High

Holy Days—*Rosh Hashanah (rosh hah-shah-NAH)*, the New Year, and *Yom Kippur (yome kih-POOR)*, the Day of Atonement. Admission tickets are required for those services, because of the capacity congregations which attend. If you apply well enough in advance, a courtesy admission ticket will very likely be given to you.

You don't have to participate in the service if you are not so inclined, although nothing happens at a Jewish service which would be contrary to Christian sensibilities.

Nina, a Jewish co-worker of whom I'm very fond, invited me to attend her son Steve's Bar Mitzvah. I was delighted to receive the invitation, until another Jewish woman in the office took me aside and suggested that I shouldn't wear my cross to synagogue. I never take off my cross. Should I decline to attend Steve's Bar Mitzvah?

No. You have every right to wear the insignia of your faith in whatever environment you find yourself. There is no reason why you should have to attend a Jewish service incognito.

A few years ago, a segment of the TV series, "All In the Family," featured a scene in which a rabbi declared the non-Jewish Archie and Edith Bunker to be members of a synagogue, because they had enrolled their Jewish niece in Hebrew school. Can people who are not Jewish join a synagogue?

Not really. In some Reform congregations, the non-Jewish spouse of a Jewish member may be permitted to join as a non-voting member. In Orthodox and Conservative synagogues, this would not be O.K.

The case of the Bunkers, in which neither Archie nor Edith were Jewish, would disqualify them for synagogue membership, no matter in which Jewish denomination.

Do you have parishes as the Catholic Church does?

No. Jews may join synagogues anywhere they wish, without regard to the areas in which they live.

From the Jewish services I have attended, I don't remember a collection or offertory being taken. Why not?

The services which you have visited probably were Sabbath services, perhaps on the occasion of a *Bar* or *Bat Mitzvah (bahr, baht MITS-vah)*, and there is no precedent for a collection plate being passed, since Jews traditionally are not supposed to handle money on the Sabbath.

Even though this restriction applies in our times to Orthodox and some Conservative Jews, the practice of collections, even at Reform services with very few exceptions, never became prevalent.

Some Reform congregations, however, have charity boxes at the doors leading to the sanctuary, where arriving or departing worshippers may drop contributions.

At daily morning and evening services in Orthodox and Conservative synagogues, with the exception of the Sabbath and holidays, it is customary to pass a charity receptacle among the worshippers.

Are Jewish families tithed?

Although the idea of tithing, setting apart a tenth of a person's income, is mentioned frequently in the Pentateuch and in the Prophetic writings of the Hebrew Bible, it is not a part of Jewish practice today.

Jews who belong to synagogues pay annual membership dues, based either on a fee established by the congregation or on a "fair share" plan based on individual family income.

In addition, Jewish people are well known for their participation in civic and Jewish philanthropies for causes in the United States as well as in Israel. However, such contributions are made on a voluntary basis and not as the result of tithing.

How is a synagogue run and financed?

The administration of a synagogue is under lay, not ecclesiastical, supervision. The members of every synagogue elect a president, vice president(s), secretary and treasurer, as well as a board of directors or trustees, all for one or two-year terms of office.

These individuals, who can be men or women, interview and engage the rabbi, cantor and educational and music directors. In the instance of hiring or renewing the rabbi, congregational confirmation may be required.

The lay leaders also engage the operations staff. Most large congregations have executive directors who are the chief operating members of the staffs. Synagogues with large memberships may staff several secretaries, a bookkeeper and a receptionist. In addition, there is a maintenance crew.

All this, of course, results in very large congregational budgets, especially when you consider that operating a weekday religious school with its faculty of professional and usually unionized teachers always spells a deficit.

Funds come from annual membership dues, which may be arbitrary, fixed amounts or based on the income of each individual family. Tuition is charged for children in the religious school. However, neither of these sources is sufficient to cover the budget.

Additional sources of revenue may include a building fund, to which each member is required to pledge a total amount, which can be paid annually, semi-annually or quarterly; an appeal for funds from the pulpit once a year at High Holy Day services, when a maximum attendance is assured; and supplementary fundraising activities by the congregation or its auxuliaries (sisterhood, men's club) such as dinner dances, ad books, bazaars, rummage sales and art shows.

Is it O.K. for Jews not to attend synagogue, or do they have to join and attend?

There is no requirement that Jews must affiliate with a synagogue, or even that they must attend religious services.

However, even though Judaism does not have a requirement comparable to the Roman Catholic obligation to attend mass, by definition a religious Jew typically attends services and, in most instances, is a synagogue member.

10

Rabbis

What is a rabbi, and what does a rabbi do?

A rabbi is a person who has been ordained at a Jewish seminary to teach, preach and interpret Judaism.

Those three words pretty much sum up a rabbi's busy schedule. The rabbi teaches Judaism to children, teen-agers and adults; officiates at religious services, preaches from the pulpit and interprets Judaism to the non-Jewish community.

The modern rabbi is also very often called upon to administer the affairs of the congregation and to be involved in fund-raising activities.

Of course, a rabbi officiates at rites of passage, including weddings and funerals.

How should I address a rabbi? I call my priest Father O'Rourke. A Lutheran neighbor refers to her minister as Pastor Schneider. I know another clergyman who is addressed as Doctor Evans.

Call a rabbi "Rabbi" and add his or her last name. A few rabbis prefer that title to be followed by their first names, as parish priests often do. The co-author of this book has T-shirts emblazoned with "Rabbi Sid."

Avoid using "Pastor" or "Father." "Doctor" is in order only if a clergy person has a doctoral degree and prefers to be addressed that way.

Sometimes, a rabbi hears himself or herself referred to as "Reverend" or "Mister" or "Ms." All wrong!

So, stick with "Rabbi."

What do you have to do to become a rabbi?

Assuming that a Jewish individual has a respectable background in Jewish studies and the Hebrew language and possesses a college degree, he or she must enroll in a recognized rabbinical seminary for a four-year course. Successful completion of seminary studies leads to ordination, and—*voila!*—one is a rabbi (or a reasonable facsimile).

Do rabbis receive a "call," like preachers?

When a member of the Christian clergy says that he or she received a "call" to the religious vocation, he or she refers to a semi-mystic experience of being summoned by God to enter upon religious service.

Rabbis do not credit divine intervention for their entrance into the rabbinate. Their motives, however, are no less special: a desire to serve God and the Jewish people, to preach and teach *Torah (toe-RAH)*.

May a person who has been converted to Judaism become a rabbi?

By all means. Once an individual has become Jewish, he or she may enjoy all the privileges and possibilities that a born Jew has. Some distinguished rabbis of the Talmudic period were converts to the Jewish faith!

Can a woman be a rabbi?

You bet! Since Rabbi Sally J. Priesand was ordained by the (Reform) Hebrew Union College—Jewish Institute of Religion—in 1972, increasing numbers of women—more than 100 to date—have become rabbis in the Reconstructionist and Reform denominations.

In 1985, the Conservative movement in Judaism began to ordain female candidates for the rabbinate.

Only Orthodox Judaism clings to the rabbi-must-be-a-male tradition.

Who hires and fires a rabbi; or, whom would a rabbi notify that he or she wants to leave a particular pulpit?

Unlike many Protestant denominations, whose synods or other governing bodies place, transfer and remove ministers from church pulpits, the relationship between a rabbi and a synagogue is a direct one. Subject often to congregational approval, the synagogue's board of directors engages the rabbi, offers a contract for his or her services for a specific period of time, and either renews the contract or terminates the rabbi's services.

However, when a congregation is seeking the services of a rabbi, it usually goes to the placement bureau of either the Reform, Conservative, Orthodox or Reconstructionist national rabbinical organizations. The placement office, in turn, submits the names and resumés of a limited number (usually three) rabbis who are available for personal interviews by the interested synagogue.

In the case you mention of a rabbi who wishes to leave his or her pulpit, both the congregation, through its officers, and the national rabbinical body would have to be notified.

Is there any kind of hierarchy among rabbis?

There is no magisterium and no hierarchy in Judaism, no monsignors, bishops, cardinals.

Most rabbis belong to a national rabbinic organization representing their particular Orthodox, Conservative, Reform or Reconstructionist denomination. These bodies have national and regional offices, staffed by executive directors. It is to these executives or to the elected leadership of the rabbinical groups that the rabbi would turn for advice and guidance.

Do the Jews have a pope?

No. Judaism has no religious hierarchy leading up to the office of pope. The State of Israel has chief rabbis, but they are not by any means in the category of popes.

Anyhow, how could you get Jews to agree upon a spokesperson? It is said that when you have two Jews, you have three opinions; or, that the only things two Jews can agree upon is how much money a third Jewish person should contribute to charity.

So, it would be an endless task waiting for the white smoke to go up, signaling "We have a pope!"

What about the chief rabbi of Israel?

The State of Israel has not one but two chief rabbis. They serve as the top religious officials in that country. One is the *Ashkenazic (ah-sh'ken-AH-zik)* Chief Rabbi, serving the Jews of European background; the other, the *Sephardic (seh-FAR-dik)* Chief Rabbi, oversees the religious needs of Israeli Jews of Oriental and Middle Eastern lineage.

The two chief rabbis are elected by their peers and colleagues and serve for stated terms in office.

Are rabbis permitted to marry?

Yes, indeed. As a matter of fact, within Orthodox Judaism one of the desired qualities for a rabbi is that he be a married man. (There are no women rabbis in the Orthodox denomination.)

Can a rabbi be divorced?

Yes.

Does a rabbi perform circumcisions?

The circumcision of a Jewish infant boy is performed by a *mohel (MO-hell)* who is specially trained for this ritual function. A rabbi need not be present, although, in Orthodox Judaism, the *mohel* might also be a rabbi.

If, instead of a *mohel,* a Jewish doctor performs the circumcision as a surgical procedure, and provided it is done on the eighth day after birth as prescribed by Jewish law, a rabbi would be present to conduct the ritual ceremony.

Are the prayers of Jews relayed to God through rabbis?

No! In Judaism there is no intermediary between the individual and God. When the Jew prays, he or she has a direct line.

A rabbi's presence on the pulpit at services in the modern synagogue may be misleading in this respect. All he or she does is to act as a kind of religious master of ceremonies. Historically, the rabbi did not even sit on the pulpit but in the first row of the congregation, ascending to the pulpit only to preach on special occasions.

This is one of the areas in which Judaism differs radically from its daughter religion, where Jesus is paraphrased as saying "...no one comes to the Father, but by me" *(John 14:6)* and in which Roman Catholics ask for the intercession of the Blessed Virgin Mary.

Do rabbis hear confession?

Not in the Catholic sense of sitting on one side of a confessional booth to hear the obligatory confessions of the faithful and to prescribe appropriate penance or absolution.

However, as pastoral counselors, rabbis are, of course, privy to the problems, if not the "confessions," of many who come to them to discuss marital discord, extra-marital affairs, abortions, drugs and other problems of men and women in contemporary society.

As in the instance of the Christian clergy, such confidences told to the rabbi remain between him or her and the person who has come and are regarded as part of a privileged relationship.

Does a rabbi wear a special uniform?

While officiating at a religious service, a rabbi customarily wears a skull cap, called a *kippa (kee-PAH)* or *yarmulke (YAHR-mool-keh)* and a prayer shawl or stole, called a *tallit (tah-LEET)*. Some Reform rabbis wear neither.

It used to be customary for rabbis to wear pulpit robes; some still do, but the practice seems to be declining.

Do rabbis wear collars?

You must be referring to the "Roman collars" worn by Roman Catholic priests and some Protestant clergy.

No, rabbis don't wear clerical collars. Shirts and ties, yes, but not collars.

Is it appropriate for a rabbi to wear jeans? How about shorts?

Sure, if he or she isn't Orthodox. The answer, as in so many other instances in this book, depends on what denomination in Jewish religion is being considered. Orthodox rabbis, for example, rarely wear informal outfits.

However, if you could look into a non-Orthodox rabbi's closet, you would find a stack of T-shirts and shorts, bathing trunks and jeans alongside the suits and skirts and robes.

For hiking, jogging, swimming and tennis, gardening and just relaxing, the rabbi will pull out the casual clothes. But comes time for formal religious services and official community appearances, and out will come the shirts, suits and dresses.

It's rumored that a few rabbis even own turquoise-studded Western ties!

When I wander through Jewish neighborhoods, I see men dressed in long, black coats and wearing wide-brimmed hats. Are they rabbis?

They might be, but more likely they are *Hassidim (khah-SEE-deem),* followers of a pietist group of Orthodox Jews which was founded in Poland in the latter decades of the 18th century. The clothes they wear is the same garb worn by men at the time the sect was organized.

Some of the men you observe wearing these garments might be Hassidic rabbis, but most of them are lay people.

Clothes do not make the rabbi!

Are rabbis permitted to have alcoholic drinks?

Yes. Wine and spirits are acceptable in Judaism. Wine is a part of the religious ritual on the Sabbath, at the Passover *seder (SAY-dare),* on the festivals of *Sukkot (soo-KOTE)* and *Shavuot (shah-voo-OTE)* and on the Jewish New Year.

Extreme moderation is, of course, recommended. The raising of a glass filled with grape or other fruit juice couldn't hurt.

I am a Catholic. A friend is a former priest who is now an attorney. He knows a rabbi who no longer serves a pulpit. This man is also an attorney; however, he still considers himself to be a rabbi. Is he?

Once a rabbi, always a rabbi. If the man you are inquiring about was ordained at a recognized Jewish theological college, he can retain the title of rabbi for so long as he wishes. If he continues to teach

Judaism—the primary function of a rabbi—formally or informally, he has not forsaken his calling.

Can a rabbi be unfrocked?

No; but he can be unsuited.

11

Symbols

On a recent trip to Los Angeles, we saw Jewish men wearing round, black hats; long, black coats; white knickers, and they had fringes hanging out of their shirttails. Do they belong to a special sect? What do their outfits represent?

What you saw were *Hassidim (khah-SEE-deem),* followers of a pious sect in Judaism which was founded in Poland in the second half of the 18th century.

Their dress is copied from the garb that the Polish gentry wore at that time. The *Hassidim* continue to favor this wardrobe to the present time, much as the Amish and other sects in our country wear quaint outfits in deference to tradition.

The fringes which you saw peeking out are a mini-version of the *tallit (tah-LEET),* the prayer shawl which Jewish men wear at worship in accord with the commandment *(Numbers 15:38–39)* to make fringes on the corners of garments to recall God's teachings.

I sometimes see Jewish men and boys wearing what look like beanies on their heads. Why? How come all Jewish people don't wear them? Why haven't I seen women wearing them?

Just as people in the Western, Christianized world remove their head coverings when entering a structure, whether it be a home, a church or an office building, Jews have developed the opposite custom and cover their heads as a sign of respect and reverence.

Very observant Jewish males keep their heads covered all the time except when they sleep. All Orthodox, most Conservative, many Reconstructionist and a few Reform Jews cover their heads when they worship, study and meet in a synagogue.

The skullcap which is worn by a man or boy (what you have called a "beanie") is called in Hebrew a *kippa (kee-PAH)* and in Yiddish a *yarmulke (YAHR-mool-keh)*.

Traditionally, women wore veils or scarfs to cover their heads. Married women wore wigs; many Orthodox women still do.

Women could wear skullcaps, too, if they want. Why not?

What does the six-pointed Star of David symbolize?

Formed by two equal-sided triangles placed opposite each other with a common center, the star goes back to very ancient times—would you believe the Bronze Age?—and was known to many cultures.

In those days, it had a kind of magical property. One theory is that the two triangles placed opposite each other is like the portrayal of yin-yang, a connecting of contradictions and opposites; therefore, a symbol of peace.

In the 19th century, Jews began to use the Star of David in decorating synagogue interiors and exteriors to identify Jewish houses of worship, in the same way that the cross indicates a church.

What are those little ornaments I have seen on the doorposts of many Jewish homes?

With regard to the teachings of the Bible, Jews are commanded to "inscribe them on the doorposts of your home and on your gates." *(Deuteronomy 6:9)* That verse, together with other brief selections from the same final book of the Pentateuch and along with the Hebrew name of God, are tucked into a small wooden or metal tube and affixed to the right doorpost as you enter a Jewish home.

This is called a *mezuza (meh-ZOO-zah),* and the observant Jew kisses it with his or her fingers when entering or leaving the house or apartment. Some Jews also place *mezuzot* (plural of *mezuza*) on the doorposts of each room in the home.

What is the meaning of the symbols many Jews wear on chains around their necks?

Some people wear the six-pointed Star of David, a symbol which also appears on many synagogue exteriors and interiors, including stained glass windows.

Another symbol consists of two Hebrew consonants which, together, spell *hai,* the Hebrew word for "life."

Still another popular symbol which is worn is a miniature *mezuza (meh-ZOO-zah),* which is described in the previous answer.

I was raised Catholic. When we were kids, when we made a promise, we would say, "Cross my heart and hope to die!" We would actually make the sign of the cross over our hearts with our fingers, sometimes just an x. Do Jews make the sign of the six-pointed Star of David over their chests?

No, we have no body language to emphasize what we are promising.

Some Jewish adults, particularly those who emigrated to the United States from Eastern Europe during the first quarter of the 20th century, impress their sincerity and truthfulness upon others by such statements as "May I never live to cross the street, if I'm not telling the truth!" "May lightning strike me if..."

Talk about guilt tripping!

12

Rites of Passage:
Growing Up Jewish

Circumcision appears to be a cruel and primitive practice. How does Judaism rationalize this, to the extent that every Jewish infant boy must undergo it?

Circumcision of the male Jewish baby is one of the most important religious requirements in Judaism. In the Hebrew language, it is called *b'rit milah (beh-REET MEE-lah),* "the covenant of circumcision," and is often known simply as the *bris (b'RIHS).*

Jewish ritual circumcision should be performed by a *mohel (MO-hell),* who uses a trustworthy, millenia-old technique which includes dabbing a cotton puff soaked in a little wine on the baby's mouth. It has an anesthetic effect; presumably, the baby feels nothing.

Why does circumcision take place on the eighth day after birth?

Genesis 17:12 in the Hebrew Bible is very specific: "At the age of eight days, every male among you...must be circumcised...."

This time period is so fixed that a Jewish ritual circumcision must take place even if the eighth day falls on the Sabbath or on *Yom Kippur (yome kih-POOR),* the Day of Atonement, unless the child has been born by Caesarian section, in which case the ceremony can be postponed to the next day. The only other exception is if the infant's health would be jeopardized.

It is worth noting that by the eighth day the coagulation time for the baby's blood is more fixed and dependable.

The practice which is followed in some hospitals of circumcising the infant on a day other than the eighth day after birth divests the surgery of any accompanying Jewish religious significance.

Many ritual circumcisions take place at home.

Do Jewish children have godparents?

In Christian practice, a godfather or godmother is one who serves as the sponsor at the baptism. Baptism is not a part of Judaism.

Godparents are officially involved only in the case of Jewish baby boys. When a Jewish boy is circumcised on the eighth day after his birth, the man who holds the baby (usually, one of the grandfathers) is designated as the *sandek (SAHN-dake)* or *kvater (k'VAH-tehr)*, and the woman who hands the baby to him is called a *sandakit (SAHN-dah-keet)* or *kvaterin (k'VAH-teh-rihn)*. The terms *kvater* and *kvaterin* derive from the German *Gevatter*, which means "godfather."

But I know Jewish girls who have godparents.

Did we say there was a law against having them?

Does a Jewish baby have anything like a christening?

Look at the word, "christening." As the name implies, the purpose of that ceremony is to baptize an infant and thereby make the baby officially Christian.

That adds up to *no* christening for a Jewish baby.

At the christening, names are assigned to Christian babies. How and when do Jewish babies get their names?

A Jewish boy is named during a ritual circumcision, known in Hebrew as a *brit milah (beh-REET MEE-lah)*, which is held on the eighth day of his life.

A Jewish baby girl is named in a special ceremony in a synagogue at the Sabbath service following her birth. In Reform congregations, the ceremony will be held when Mom can join Dad at the service.

Also in the Reform practice, if a baby boy is circumcised in a hospital surgical procedure without an accompanying religious ritual, he may be assigned a Jewish name in a synagogue ceremony.

What do you mean by a "Jewish name"? I attended a circumcision ceremony where the boy got two names. Why?

It happens to most Jewish boys and girls. They receive one or two Hebrew names in addition to their English names.

The Hebrew names are those by which the child, and later the adult, is identified in religious school and ceremonies such as Bar or Bat Mitzvah, when called to the reading of Scripture at a synagogue service, and during the marriage ceremony.

The Hebrew name links the Jewish child with his or her parents, grandparents and great-grandparents, and with the generations of Jews who have preceded them, stretching way back to the Biblical patriarchs and matriarchs.

What is a Bar Mitzvah?

A *Bar Mitzvah (bahr MITS-vah)* is both a person and a ceremony.

When a Jewish boy reaches the age of 13 years, he is considered to be a *Bar Mitzvah,* which is roughly translated as a "son of a good deed," who can be held responsible for carrying out God's commandments.

Since the 15th century, 13-year-old Jewish boys have been inducted into the adult Jewish community in formal synagogue ceremonies.

This induction or initiation event itself is also called a *Bar Mitzvah,* short for *"Bar Mitzvah* ceremony." For the first time in his young life, the boy gets up before the congregation and reads in the original Hebrew a portion of the *Torah (toe-RAH)* from one of the first five books of the Bible as well as an excerpt from the writings of one of the Hebrew Prophets.

The boy spends several years studying the Hebrew language, Bible, Jewish history and prayers to prepare for his *Bar Mitzvah.*

Why does a Bar Mitzvah take place at 13?

Centuries ago, Jewish sources determined that a boy attained legal and religious majority the day after his 13th birthday anniversary.

On that special day, the boy became a *Bar Mitzvah (bahr MITS-vah)*, a "son of a good deed" commanded by God, in the eyes of the Jewish community. The *Bar Mitzvah* ceremony simply made the whole event public.

While the ceremony customarily is held at 13 years of age, it can be held any time after those years. Today, many adult Jews who never went through the ceremony when they entered their teen years to take part in it as middle-aged or older men and women.

However, it is not required that a person go through a *Bar Mitzvah* ceremony to be considered a Jew.

You only mention boys.

A girl becomes a *Bat Mitzvah (baht MITS-vah)*, "daughter of a good deed" commanded by God. That is also the name of the ceremony in which she reads a portion of the Bible in the synagogue for the first time.

It took almost 1700 years for Jewish girls to be recognized as total persons and deserving of a special ceremony. The first such *Bat Mitzvah* for a girl was celebrated in 1927 in New York City.

Many people say that a child has been "barmitzvahed" or "batmitzvahed." That's wrong. He or she "has become a Bar/Bat Mitzvah," is the correct way of phrasing it.

Can you suggest an appropriate Bar Mitzvah gift? Is it a good idea to give money?

Select a gift for a *Bar Mitzvah* boy or a *Bat Mitzvah* girl which reflects the nature of the occasion, a spiritual one. Highlight this spiritual emphasis even when the party which follows the service in the synagogue may assume a highly materialistic and hedonistic character—emphasizing the "bar" more than the *mitzvah*.

The idea should be to reinforce a strong value system for the 13-year-old recipient who is on the brink of adulthood.

Books, records and cassettes, particularly those with Jewish content, make great gifts. So do Jewish artifacts. Comb Jewish book stores in larger cities and synagogue gift shops for these.

Try a tape recorder, portable radio, tickets to a concert or ballet.

How about a gift that stresses creativity? A gift certificate for pottery lessons, camera equipment, film and developing, a photo album, slide trays.

No, giving money or writing a check is not a good idea. It doesn't reflect any thought or concern by you as donor about the gift. Besides, the "envelope collection" tends to turn the *Bar* or *Bat Mitzvah* into a business venture, complete with a running tally—what the kids call "collecting the loot."

What do children study in "Hebrew school"?

They learn to read, write and, hopefully, understand Hebrew, the language of the Bible and Jewish prayerbook and the language of the State of Israel.

The boys and girls also study Jewish history, beliefs, personalities, customs and ceremonies, and holiday observances.

The classes are usually held in synagogues, anywhere from two to four times a week after public school hours.

Are there Jewish parochial schools?

In Jewish all-day schools, children receive both religious and secular education.

Since the term, "parochial," literally refers to a Roman Catholic parish, Jews prefer to call theirs "day schools."

13

Rites of Passage:
Getting Married,
Getting Unmarried

Her father always gives the bride away in Christian weddings, but in Jewish weddings I've attended both parents walk the bride down the aisle. The groom's parents walk him down the aisle, too. Why?

In the Protestant marriage ritual, the minister asks, "Who gives this woman away?" and the bride's father responds with, "I do." Since this responsibility is assigned to the bride's father, he alone escorts her down the aisle and presents her to her bridegroom.

Judaism sees the wedding ceremony as an occasion for both pairs of parents, the bride's and the bridegroom's, to escort their respective children to the marriage canopy. The parents then remain standing beside the canopy while the rabbi conducts the ceremony.

Why do the bride and groom stand under a canopy at a Jewish wedding?

The most credible explanation is that the canopy symbolizes the bridal chamber in which the marriage will be consummated.

The canopy is called a *huppa (KHOO-pah)*. Covered with a material such as velvet, it is suspended over the heads of the bride and bridegroom and held up by four poles, which can be supported by four individuals or can be fastened to the ground.

At military weddings in modern Israel, the *huppa* is usually a *tallit (tah-LEET)*, a prayer shawl held up by four rifles.

In the United States, the *huppa* is typically festooned with flowers.

Why does a bridegroom break a glass by stepping on it at the end of a Jewish wedding ceremony? Why doesn't the bride do this, too?

This custom, which inspires more questions than most other Jewish practices, probably goes back to an ancient belief, not held by Jews alone, that the abrupt introduction of noise into a festive occasion serves to drive away evil spirits who would destroy the happiness of the moment.

Other examples where glass is shattered on festive occasions: the breaking of a bottle against a ship's hull at a launching; the smashing of a wine glass after a toast. For noise at a joyous time, how about the firecrackers on the Chinese New Year?

Jewish tradition relates the ritual to a reminder of the destruction of the Temple in Jerusalem.

In any case, the sobering sound of glass being broken serves to interrupt the gaiety, even if only momentarily, and to remind the wedding participants and guests that there is unhappiness and suffering in the world which must not be forgotten even at that joyous hour.

The function is assigned to the bridegroom most likely because it emphasizes the "macho" conception of a male in a sexist society, although it might be impractical for a bride, usually in her white gown and train, to have to step on a glass.

Most non-Jewish wedding ceremonies are typically conducted in church or at home. Every Jewish wedding I have attended has been held in a hotel. Why not in a synagogue?

Why not, indeed! You have touched upon one of the unfortunate aspects of American Jewish social practice.

During the Middle Ages, Jewish marriage ceremonies were held in synagogues or in the open on property adjacent to the synagogue.

There is no valid reason why the Jewish wedding ceremony, as distinguished from the reception, should not be held in the sacred setting of the synagogue or in the nostalgic environs of the family home, rather than in the impersonal and secular surroundings of a commercial hotel.

Would it be proper to ask a Jewish friend to be my best man? The wedding will take place in a Catholic church.

No problem, provided that your friend will not have to genuflect or otherwise participate in the wedding liturgy.

Mazal Tov (mah-ZAHL tove)! Congratulations and Good Luck!

I've always heard that Jewish people enjoy a very warm and close family life, but I'm meeting many Jews who are divorced. What's happening?

What's happening is the same thing that happens to other ethnic groups in the United States, when the earlier generation of immigrants passes on and is replaced by American-born men and women who have become, to use the sociologist's term, "acculturated."

The old ways are sloughed off, unfortunately including the strong sense of family and respect for the aged, among other values.

At the same time, we have to recognize, when we speak of divorce, that among the immigrants women were forced to play a subservient role, while men were dominant, "macho." As women have become more assertive, traditional prohibition against divorce has weakened, and more and more people have taken advantage of it.

Divorce is only the tip of the iceberg. The crumbling of the strong Jewish family, with its bonds of love and loyalty, is the real tragedy.

Career, social and economic pressures tug at the family's security. As parents community-hop around the country to follow increasingly impressive job offers, they and their children are snatched from the warmth and roots provided by grandparents, uncles, aunts and cousins.

Divorce is not intrinsically bad. It may be, and often is, the only way out of an unwise early marriage between two immature young people whose disparate and conflicting value systems become more apparent with the passing years.

Divorce is certainly called for in instances of child abuse and spousal abuse, physical or emotional.

When professional counseling verifies that incompatibility has resulted in a truly irretrievable marriage, divorce becomes a positive action.

Then, Judaism doesn't frown upon divorce?

No. In Orthodox and Conservative Judaism, however, there is a requirement that a civil divorce be accompanied by the husband granting a *geht,* a religious "bill of divorcement" *(Deuteronomy 24:3)* to his former wife before either one may remarry.

Since the woman cannot initiate the proceedings leading to the granting of a religious divorce, she is at the mercy of her former husband if he proves uncooperative, as frequently is the case.

14

Rites of Passage: When All Is Said and Done

Is a rabbi called upon to deliver last rites?

In accord with the Biblical promise that a person who confesses sins or faults and gives them up will find mercy *(Proverbs 28:13),* Judaism provides a ritual of confession which the dying person can recite before the end comes.

The brief ceremony, which provides for the individual confession of transgressions, ends poignantly with the dying person's last words being the classic statement of Jewish belief, the *Shema (sheh-MAH),* "Hear, O Israel, the Lord is our God, the Lord is one!" *(Deuteronomy 6:4)*

Neither a rabbi nor anyone else has to be involved in this final act, except that the dying person usually is so weak that someone has to be on hand to assist. That someone may be a rabbi.

A rabbi does not play the role that a Catholic priest does when he administers the sacrament of extreme unction to a person *in extremis,* that is, dying.

Do Jews allow autopsies?

Although there is no prohibition against autopsies in the Bible or post-Biblical literature, Orthodox Jewish authorities have become increasingly outspoken in their opposition to the practice.

They base their opposition on the Talmudic principle that dissecting a body is a violation of the dignity of the dead person and that a body should be buried intact, to await resurrection with the coming of the Messiah.

Reform and Conservative Judaism, although less vehemently opposed, generally take the view that autopsies should be performed only when and if they would result in a demonstrable benefit to living people.

This view results from the increasingly prevalent practice by authorities in teaching hospitals and medical schools of pressuring families to permit post mortems on loved ones merely to fill a spurious quota.

How about embalming?

Judaism is opposed to embalming, which removes the blood and, possibly, some of the organs from the body. This opposition stems from the traditional Jewish view that the body must be buried intact to await bodily resurrection which will accompany the coming of the Messiah. Orthodox Jews believe this so intensely that in the instance of a person who has a limb amputated the severed limb should be buried and reunited with the rest of the body when the individual dies.

The traditional attitude against embalming is strengthened in modern times by the recognition that embalming is a cosmetic procedure and not a long-term preservative of the remains.

Do Jews permit cremation?

Cremation is contrary to Orthodox Jewish law. Traditional Judaism is opposed to anything that hastens the destruction of the body, which should await the resurrection that will come with the Messiah. Further, cremation was viewed as a pagan rite originated in the days of fire worship.

Conservative Judaism, while respecting the traditional law, varies in the extent of its opposition to cremation.

Reform Judaism has no objection to the practice.

Is it appropriate to send flowers to a Jewish funeral?

It is not. All denominations within Jewish religion agree that the money spent for floral displays, which are then heaped upon the new grave to wilt and wither, is wasted.

Judaism has always believed that the best way to honor the memory of a person who has passed away and, by so doing, help comfort the survivors, is to contribute to charity, to causes which will advance the ideals in which the deceased believed.

It is, therefore, very appropriate to contribute to institutions and movements which help people, animals, the environment, education and the arts.

Can a non-Jewish spouse be buried next to a Jewish husband or wife in a Jewish cemetery?

Yes, in the case of a non-Jewish husband or wife or a close relation. No, in the instance of a non-Jew who is not related.

Why don't Jews have visitation and viewing in the chapel the night before a funeral?

Some Jews do arrange for chapel visitation the night before the funeral of a loved one, but it is contrary to Jewish tradition and is generally not done.

Jews believe that a genuine tribute to the deceased is to take time off from your schedule to attend the funeral service rather than to create a social occasion by having a convenient get-together in advance of the last rites.

I have attended several Jewish funerals and have noticed that the caskets are opened before or after but not during the funeral service, or not opened at all. Why?

Jews do not believe that viewing a corpse serves any purpose except a morbid one. We want to remember the deceased as he or she was as a living, vibrant personality.

The cosmetic and hair-styling attempts which go into trying to make the corpse "attractive" run counter to the Jewish concept of recognizing the reality of death rather than trying to conceal it.

I have just returned home after attending the funeral service for the father of one of my closest friends, who is Jewish. As a teen-ager, I spent as much time in Lester's house as I did my own; and I liked his dad very much. Anyhow, when the service ended in the funeral chapel, and we were ushered by the coffin on the way out to the burial site, I did what I have been trained to do as a Catholic. I knelt in front of the casket for a few seconds, crossed myself and said a silent prayer for the repose of Mr. Samuels' soul. Some of the Jewish people present seemed to look strangely at me. Did I do wrong?

Not at all. You were paying a sincere tribute to the memory of someone you knew and cared for in the manner dictated by your particular faith. Only an insecure member of another religion would object.

One of the fellows who works with me lost his mother. He said he would be out of the office for several days, because he had to "sit *shiva.*" What is that?

The *shiva (SHIH-vah)* is a seven-day period beginning immediately after a funeral in which the mourners remain home and receive condolence calls. It is broken only by the the Sabbath, from sundown Friday to sundown Saturday, or by the intervention of a Jewish holiday.

Some Jews cut the *shiva* period down to three days.

Do Jews believe in Heaven and Hell?

The Hebrew Bible says nothing about life after death. The suggestions of an afterlife in the books of Isaiah and Daniel very likely are to be associated with the coming of the Messiah.

One traditional Jewish view conceives of the soul at death descending into a pit called *Sheol (sh'OLE)* where it remains until the resurrection comes with the arrival of the Messiah. Another view is that the soul stands in judgment before God immediately after a person dies.

In the same folklore, another name for Hell, in addition to *Sheol,* is *Gehinnom* (in the Gospels, the Greek name, *Gehenna,* is used). *Gehinnom (geh-HEE-nahm)* literally means "valley of Hinnom," a garbage dump near Jerusalem where trash was constantly burned.

Jewish folklore is rich in references to Heaven, which is called *Gan Eden (gahn AY-den),* Hebrew for the Garden of Eden or Paradise, a place in which the disembodied souls of those who led exemplary lives on earth enjoy eternal life.

When a Jew dies, we pray that his or her soul will rest in *Gan Eden,* sometimes referred to as "the world to come" or "the academy on high."

Do Jews believe in Life Everlasting?

Yes, in the sense that only the physical body dies and is placed in the earth or crypt. The spirit lives on in the thoughts of those who remember. "Love is as strong as death," says the Biblical *Song of Songs (8:6).*

The past, those who lived before us, lives on in us. The great Jewish philosopher, Spinoza, said that every life is like a stone cast into a lake, setting off ripples. When a relative or close friend passes away, he or she becomes a part of us, for the impact of his or her life upon our lives continues through the miracle of memory.

Do Jews believe in resurrection? In the original body?

One of the oldest passages in the traditional Jewish prayer book praises God "Who resurrects the dead." Orthodox Judaism believes in bodily resurrection, one of the phenomena which will occur with the coming of the Messiah.

This belief has an interesting side consequence. If an Orthodox Jew loses a limb through surgery or an accident, the limb is buried temporarily. When the individual who lost the limb dies, the limb is reburied with him or her, so that, when the Messiah arrives, the resurrected body will be intact.

This is also one of the reasons why traditional Jews frown upon embalming and autopsies. Removal of blood from the body after death, or the disfigurement of any of its organs during a post-mortem, would be contrary to the idea of bodily resurrection.

Non-Orthodox Jews do not believe in bodily resurrection.

Do Jews believe in ghosts?

Jewish teaching is opposed to believing in ghosts. In spite of this, incidents of contacting the spirits of the dead are recorded in Biblical times and, later, in Talmudic times.

In *I Samuel 28:7–19,* we read that Saul, using the witch of Endor as a medium, called up the spirit of the dead Samuel to advise him in dealing with the Philistines.

Because of official Jewish opposition to trafficking with the dead, there is an absence of detailed literature on the subject. A few observations have been made by Jewish scholars. For example, you can question the dead only within the first year of their demise, because their physical remains probably have not yet completely decomposed. By the way, when summoned, we are informed that the ghost rises from the grave feet first.

While interrogating the physical manifestation of the deceased is prohibited, appealing to the memory of the dead is acceptable. Jewish customs have included visiting the graves of immediate family members for spiritual support. A bridal couple often make the trek to the cemetery shortly before the wedding to solicit approval for the forthcoming nuptials.

In the *Kabbalah (kah-BAH-lah),* the literature of Jewish mysticism which is not a part of normative, universally-accepted Judaism, ghosts and the occult play much more respectable roles. For instance, the Kabbalah mentions "automatic writing" and the "levitating table," two of the phenomena associated with ghosts and spiritualism.

What is the significance of the little candles that sometimes burn in glasses or tiny cans in Jewish homes?

On each anniversary of the death of a member of the immediate family, Jewish people kindle a memorial candle, which burns in the home for 24 hours.

The candle is known as a *Jahrzeit (YAHR-tseit)* light. The Yiddish word means "a year's time."

15

Delicate Areas

Why do so many Jewish young people join cults?

We have no exact statistics for the number of Jewish young persons who have joined the Hare Krishna, the Unification Church (the so-called "Moonies"), "Jews for Jesus," "Messianic Jews," "Hebrew Christians." However, it has been estimated that Jews comprise between 12 and 15 percent of the overall membership of the more than 3,000 religious cults in the United States. The number is much greater than the proportion of Jews to the general population.

The attraction of these groups for young Jews has little to do with their religious or theological outlook but is a sad commentary on established Jewish institutions in the United States, among them the synagogue.

Every human being needs to feel that he or she belongs, to feel secure, to feel joy in sharing with others, to feel confident about himself or herself.

From the testimony of young Jewish people who have been "deprogrammed" after belonging to cults, as well as from those who explain why they remain in such groups, we know that the major appeal the cults offer to the lonely and alienated person in our "age of anxiety" is a warm, affectionate and immediate acceptance into the "family," without regard to status.

Too often, the modern synagogue appears not to provide an environment of comfort for the lonely single and the person who has not found his or her niche in the social order. The American synagogue seems to cater to the upper middle-class family unit: husband, wife and children. Further, the synagogue fragments its membership into men's clubs, sisterhoods, auxiliaries for "under 35," "over 35," "teen-agers," "senior citizens."

Sometimes, it seems that we have forgotten God's command to remember the stranger, "for you were strangers in the land of Egypt." *(Exodus 23:9)* The forgotten stranger is easily seduced by cults.

Nevertheless, a warm and stimulating synagogue environment alone cannot insure that a young person will remain loyal to Judaism.

The home, too, must bask in a Jewish atmosphere.

Sadly, many parents, either because they lack Jewish education, or because they are preoccupied with the economic and social pressures of our fast-paced, rapidly-shifting technological society, assign the family's entire Jewish experience to the synagogue. They neglect to provide Jewish-adorned memories and Jewish family togetherness.

So, the children perceive the synagogue as the place they must go "to be Jewish."

For the Jewish experience to be dynamic, it must be fortified at home.

Children are very intelligent. If the family joins a synagogue and remains just long enough to celebrate a Bar or Bat Mitzvah, the youngsters will perceive the whole charade as socially expedient.

If the child is directed to attend Hebrew School while the parents themselves do not practice Judaism, he or she will perceive Judaism as something to be endured only by children.

In too many instances, there is no Jewish affiliation, no ties to a synagogue. The child then assumes no particular Jewish identity.

Jewish parents must ask themselves:
• Are they Jewish role models?
• Are the holidays observed in meaningful or superficial ways?
• Are *Rosh Hashanah (rosh hah-shah-NAH)* and *Yom Kippur (yome kih-POOR)* occasions to drop in on synagogue services and show off Fall wardrobes, or times when parents can guide their children in examining their lives?
• Is *Hanukkah (KHAH-noo-kah)* a mad scramble to open presents and gobble up treats, or is it a time to reflect on what religious freedom means?
• Are Jewish children given memories of a *seder (SAY-dare)*, Passover banquet, in which the contrasts between slavery and freedom are dramatized, or does the *seder* become just a gastronomic orgy?

• Is the home one in which good deeds, "acts of loving-kindness," or material possessions are counted?

Children know. They know when their home is embellished with Jewish books and tapes. In a home which is a storehouse of Judaism for a family which delights in its heritage, a child can count on the warm glow, security and continuity of Sabbath dinners, holiday observances and sharing of Jewish culture.

These youngsters grow up knowing that they are born with a religion which offers humane values, warmth and love.

Confident and secure in their Jewish identity, they need look no further.

What is "Zionism"? Is there any truth to the charge made by Arabs that Zionism is racism?

The Zionist movement was founded at the end of the 19th century to mobilize Jews all over the world in order to influence public opinion to create a homeland in Palestine for the Jewish people.

The right of those Jews who wished to return to their ancient homeland was first given recognition by a government on November 2, 1917, when Great Britain, with the concurrence of the United States Congress, declared that it looked with favor upon the Zionist goal.

Zionist efforts resulted in the creation of the State of Israel in 1948. There are Jews who believe that Zionism requires that its adherents settle in Israel, while others who call themselves Zionists feel it sufficient to support the State of Israel by visiting it, contributing money to its development and lobbying for it on a political level.

In any case, there is nothing "racist" at all about Zionism. That is a charge fabricated by enemies of the State of Israel and of the Zionist movement.

What gave Zionists the right to pick a country, announce they wanted it, kick out the residents and create a new nation?

Zionists did not "pick a country" capriciously or arbitrarily. Palestine was the ancient homeland of the Jewish people in which some Jews have resided ever since Biblical days, when God promised Moses: "I will bring you into the land which I swore to give to Abraham, Isaac and Jacob, and I will give it to you for a possession...." (Exodus 6:8)

It was in that land that the First and Second Jewish Commonwealths were based. It was there, the country known by Jews as *Erets Yisrael (EH-retz yihs-rah-EHL)*, the Land of Israel, that the Prophets preached. Even after the majority had been exiled by the Romans in 70 C.E., Jews continued for 2,000 years to mourn for Zion and pray for their return to it.

Throughout those centuries, Palestine was never an independent Arab state. In area, it forms only 1/23 of total Arab land holdings; the remaining area of 22/23 of Arab lands is sparsely settled.

In the last decades of the 19th century, the Jewish settlement in the Holy Land was augmented by thousands of new arrivals, young Jews from Eastern Europe who came to build and to be rebuilt. They drained the marshes, made the desert bloom, established schools and hospitals and formed cooperatives.

In November, 1947, the Arab world rejected the proposal of the United Nations to partition Palestine into Arab and Jewish states. The following May, when the British Mandate over Palestine came to an end, the armies of six Arab countries invaded the Holy Land from three sides to destroy the newly-proclaimed State of Israel.

The Israelis did not, in turn, "kick out" the Arab residents of the country. The resident Arabs in vast numbers heeded the propaganda of their leaders, led by the infamous, alleged friend and supporter of Hitler, the Mufti of Jerusalem, to flee the land or face a fancied annihilation by the Israeli army.

This is how the Arab refugee problem was originally created. It has continued throughout these decades, because the Arab states refuse to absorb the refugees, who are their brother and sister Arabs, although they have plenty of land. The Arab politicians prefer to keep the hundreds and thousands of their fellow Arabs in camps in order to use them as showpieces for wheeling and dealing on the international political scene.

Is every Jew a citizen of Israel?

According to the Law of the Return, which was adopted shortly after the State of Israel was founded in 1948, every Jew, from any country, who decides to live in Israel is automatically granted Israeli citizenship. The law is based on the theory that he or she is simply returning to the homeland from which his or her ancestors were exiled 2,000 years ago.

Of course, the State of Israel also has Moslem and Christian citizens. Non-Jewish immigrants to Israel have to go through a naturalization procedure similar to that in other countries.

If American Jews are so attached to Israel, why don't they move there?

The Land of Israel, the Holy Land, plays a part in Jewish religion and history which is without precedent among other peoples. It is the land where the Hebrew Bible was written, the place where the Patriarchs Abraham, Isaac and Jacob lived, where the Hebrew Prophets gave their messages to the world.

After World War II, this land of Israel was the only country in the world to which the homeless Jews, survivors of Hitler's Holocaust, could go. These "tempest-tossed" Jews weren't welcome in any other country, including, sadly, our own United States.

There has been a strong commitment to Israel by the American Jewish community, especially since the Second World War. This commitment urges American Jews to lobby for Israel, provide financial support and tour the country.

British Jews, French Jews, South American Jews, Canadian Jews—Jews from all around the globe do the same.

At the same time, American Jews are thoroughly at home in and loyal to the United States. With few exceptions, they have no desire to exercise their option to live permanently in the ancient homeland.

The late Louis D. Brandeis, Justice of the Supreme Court of the United States and leader of American Zionism, the movement to rebuild the Jewish homeland, once said that the love for the United States and love for what is today the State of Israel cannot be contrasted, because they are like the love one has for one's mother and the love one has for one's husband or wife.

Both are valid; one does not exclude the other.

I have heard many Jews speak up for animal rights, but I have heard others take a negative position. I know Jews who support the women's movement, while others scoff at it. The same is true of gay rights and the anti-nuclear movement. What are the official Jewish stands on these issues?

There are no official Jewish positions on controversial, contemporary issues such as those you've mentioned.

What happens is that individual rabbis and other Jewish leaders reach into the Bible and Talmud and select passages which they interpret as supporting their views.

During the Civil War, rabbis, along with non-Jewish clergy, lined up on both sides of the slavery debate, quoting Biblical verses to justify their respective, and often contradictory, positions.

Progressive Jews tend to shape their views in terms of the Prophets of Israel, who preached justice, mercy and compassion. So it is no surprise that Jews are highly visible in the battles for animal rights, gay rights and women's rights and in the anti-nuke movement.

Are Jews allowed to practice birth control?

There is no objection to birth control within the Conservative, Reform and Reconstructionist denominations. Orthodox Jewish authorities oppose the use of male contraceptives, citing the Biblical admonition against "wasting of seed." *(Genesis 38:9)*

In the contemporary American scene, birth control is not practiced among many very observant Orthodox Jews, except for medical reasons, in deference to the Biblical command to "be fertile and increase." *(Genesis 1:28)*

In all groups, there are those who maintain that Jews should be an exception to the goal of "zero population growth," because they have a responsibility to replenish the world Jewish population, which has been decimated by the murder of six million Jews in the Nazi Holocaust.

Does the Jewish religion permit abortion?

Yes, but there is no uniform Jewish position.

The more traditional (Orthodox) stand is that the fetus is a part of the mother's body until the head is born, when it becomes an individual in his or her own right. It follows, then, that the mother's health while carrying the fetus is a consideration for abortion.

Within the liberal (Reform, Reconstructionist) religious Jewish community, there are many who advocate abortion-on-demand and who would agree with the contemporary feminist position that a woman should have control over her own body.

Why can't Jews be like everybody else?

To answer, again, a question with a question: Who is "everybody else," and what is "everybody else" like?

If we assume that, because you most likely live in a North American community, "everybody else" is a WASP, a White, Anglo-Saxon Protestant (or Catholic), the answer has to be, once more, in the form of a question: Why? Why is it desirable to have Jews—or anyone else, for that matter—be like everybody else? What's so desirable about uniformity?

Totalitarian states place a high premium on conformity and everyone being like everyone else. Democracy prizes unity in diversity.

Because Jews are a minority in this country and in the Western World and follow a religion which differs in theology and ritual from the majority Christian faith, and because they are part of a long history and culture which are different from the Anglo Saxon variety, they will continue to be different.

That's the price Jews have to pay for the survival of their people and its faith. It doesn't mean that Jews or Judaism are better than other folk or other beliefs...but different, yes!

Why are Jews clannish?

Clannishness, in any group, is the outgrowth of being a part of a minority, feeling left out or not belonging, sometimes feeling inferior. People who feel left out join together to seek solace.

It is very natural for individuals to be more comfortable among those whom they feel are their "in-group," whether it be social, ethnic or religious.

This has given rise to what has been described as the "5 o'clock shadow" in the American social scene, where people of varying creeds and colors work together each weekday, but when the office or factory closes at the end of the work period they scurry back to their religious, racial or ethnic enclaves and do not interact with each other until the next weekday morning.

Clannishness may be the price for the desire of a group to be different and to retain its distinctive cultural and religious practices.

This clannishness is not to be attributed to Jews alone, by any means. As a matter of fact, Jews tend to be very outgoing and gregarious. It is, rather, a product of the American social scene with its history of restrictive housing clauses, university quotas, discrimination in the executive office suite.

I am troubled by certain words that Jewish people sometimes use when they speak of a non-Jew: *"goy," "shiksah," "shaygitz," "shvartzeh."* When these names are spoken in a facetious manner, I never know whether they are really denigrating and insulting.

Goy (pl. *GOY-ihm)* is a legitimate Hebrew word. It is found frequently in the Hebrew Bible, where it means simply "people" or "nation"— Jewish as well as non-Jewish. In *Exodus 19:6,* God addresses the Israelites as being potentially "a kingdom of priests and a holy nation *(goy kadosh)."*

The terms *shiksah* and *shaygitz* are Yiddish, the vernacular of Jews in pre-Holocaust Eastern Europe. They refer, respectively, to a non-Jewish woman or girl and man or boy.

Shvartz is Yiddish (from the German) for "black," in this instance a Black person. (By the way, a Black person can convert to Judaism, the same as any non-Jew. The *Beta Yisrael (BAY-tah yihs-rah-AYL),* also known as the *Falashas (fah-LAH-shahs),* the "Black Jews of Ethiopia" who were brought to the State of Israel in the mid-1980s, trace their ancestry to King Solomon and the Queen of Sheba and practice a modified form of Judaism.)

None of these words is in itself disparaging. Like any names, however, the question of whether they are pejorative has to be determined by the context in which they are used.

Isn't it snobbery for Jews to consider themselves the Chosen People?

Even though the term, "God's Chosen People," has been applied to the Jewish people, very few Jews go around considering themselves to be superior because of it. If they do, it is not because of that designation but for the same sin of pride that makes members of other religious, ethnic and racial groups think that they are better than members of other groups.

The concept of being God's Chosen People never meant that Jews were superior, but rather that the Jewish people had been selected to carry the idea of One God and God's word to the peoples of the earth.

Jews were to be, as the Bible puts it, "a kingdom of priests and a holy nation." *(Exodus 19:6)*

Jews were chosen, in other words, to set the example. By so doing, they were asking for trouble, and Jewish history illustrates that trouble is what they got in the form of persecution.

The Reconstructionist movement, which is the newest denomination in Jewish religion, has categorically rejected the Chosen People concept and eliminated any liturgical references to it.

My Jewish co-worker, Lillian, gets Christmas and New Year's Day off, just as I do. She also takes off the Jewish New Year, the Day of Atonement and the first day of Passover. She openly brags that she spends these days shopping and going to movies. Is that fair?

No. Lillian is taking advantage of her employer's decency in granting her time off to observe the Jewish holidays you mention on the assumption that she will celebrate the holidays and not the department store sale racks and matinee specials.

It's pathetic that Lillian can't get more out of her religion than a few days off.

I am familiar with emirs and kings, marquesses and sultans, contessas and dukes; but, please tell me: What is a Jewish Princess?

The full designation is "Jewish American Princess" (the acronym is JAP), and it is supposed to describe a spoiled, hedonistic, self-centered young Jewish woman in the United States who has been pampered and over-indulged by her upper-middle class or wealthy parents. In turn, she is reputedly out to snare a husband who will continue to indulge her.

From this description, you see, there are no religious qualifications. The tragedy of over-indulged but underloved children, who bask in materialism instead of humanitarian values, crosses religious and ethnic lines.

You don't have to be Jewish to qualify.

Be careful! Like all stereotypes, that of the "Jewish American

Princess" is very faulty. Just as the delineation of the Jewish Mother by novelists on the American scene did a disservice to most of the dedicated Jewish mothers, so the satires on the JAP may be a product of a subtle anti-Semitism or, on the part of authors who themselves are Jewish, of self-hatred.

I have heard that Jews control the international banking industry. How did Jews become the powerful financiers of the world?

They don't, and they didn't.

In 1983, a survey conducted by the attorney general of New York State proved that seven of New York City's biggest banks had almost no Jews in top executive posts, although Jews constitute 50 percent of that city's college graduates.

Similarly, a 1976 study in Massachusetts revealed that only 1.1 percent of bank executive positions were held by Jews.

In Philadelphia, only 4.6 percent of top bank officers were Jews, according to a 1982 survey.

Time magazine declared that "... Jews view the [banking] industry as one of the last bastions of discrimination against them." *(11/25/74)*

But statistics can be used to justify any position; "figures lie, and liars figure." The point is that whether Jews play a small or major role in U.S. or international banking circles has nothing to do with the popular canard by anti-Semites that Jews dominate the industry. The charge is always accompanied by buzz words such as "control" and "conspiracy."

The story of how some Jews became involved in the business of money historically is a fascinating one. It was one of the few occupations they were permitted to enter in medieval Europe, because the church banned its followers from lending money for interest.

The rise of the Rothschild financial empire in England and on the Continent, Warburg Bank of Hamburg and Amsterdam, Lazard Freres bank of Paris, Israel Moses Seif Banks of Italy and, in the United States, Goldman, Sachs, Lehman Bros., and Kuhn, Loeb is a story of institutions which have played, on the whole, a commendable role in international finance—certainly a far cry from the sinister role which Jew-haters would ascribe to them.

I haven't had the guts to ask this publicly, but where do Jews get their instinct for making money?

This is an intriguing question, because it supposes that Jews—all Jews—have this talent.

The answer is that if you look at the Jewish population, with its share of families struggling, like everyone else, to make ends meet, worried about inflation, interest rates, the cost of living, job security, etc., the query vanishes in the presence of reality.

Most dramatically, the presence of an alarming number of Jews living near or below the poverty level in every metropolis would indicate that the "instinct" can't be counted on.

Truth to tell, this is one of those myths that have been popularly held for a long time, similar to the legends that all Scots are thrifty or all Blacks shiftless. Even though these are nothing more than myths, people have found them comfortable to retain and, what is worse, pass on to their children to bolster their prejudices.

Do you actually mean that there are poor Jews?

You bet! Take a look at America's—in fact, the world's—largest Jewish community, metropolitan New York City, with a Jewish population of 1,735,000.

According to a study which was released as 1984 drew to a close, there were about 144,000 Jews living below the federal poverty guidelines. A visit to 68,000 Jewish homes in New York City found them to be in conditions of poverty.

Most of that city's poor are children and working-age adults. These non-elderly poor constitute about 70 percent of all poor Jews and about half of all poor Jewish households in the Big Apple.

Now, turn your attention to Greater Los Angeles in the '80s. With more than half a million Jews, the City of Angels contains the second largest Jewish population of any city in the world.

When the 1980s began, 13 percent of the slightly more than 500,000 Jewish residents of Tinseltown had an income of less than $6,000 per year, while 8 percent had an annual income ranging between $6,000 and $9,000.

In the glamor capital of the Pacific Coast, more than one out of every five Jews was living at the poverty line!

It has been asserted that between 20 and 25 percent of all Jews in the United States live below the poverty level.

I've always thought it a bit strange that Jews have been accused of controlling the international money scene at the same time that they are charged with having many communists in their ranks. Are there a lot of Jewish communists?

Exaggerated charges about Jews being communists stem from two sources. The first is Karl Marx's "Jewish connection," which reasons that, if the founder of the theory of communism was Jewish, many of its followers must be Jewish, too.

Wrong, all the way around! Actually, the Jewish-born parents of the social philosopher and journalist who fathered communism were baptized in 1817, the year before Karl was born.

Karl Marx was officially baptized a Christian when he was 6 years old.

Secondly, anti-Semites enjoy flinging slogans about Jews being communists to hawk their Jews-as-evil image.

Remember, communist societies confined by barbed wire and suffocated by tyrannical governments and repressive laws would not appeal to Jews who have struggled for freedom and social justice.

The 1,630,000 Jews living in the Soviet Union constitute the third largest concentration of Jews in the world, next to the United States and Israel. Their spiritual survival is being systematically strangled, their contact with the State of Israel and the rest of world Jewry prohibited. Their future under the communist dictatorship of the U.S.S.R. is a bleak one.

To talk to some Jewish people, you would think that the Holocaust was the only tragedy in history. Don't they know that other people have suffered, that others have been massacred?

The horrendous immensity of the eradication of six million Jewish adults and children at the hands of the Nazis during the period just preceding and during World War II which we call the Holocaust is without precedent in its magnitude and thoroughness in all of recorded history.

The loss of grandparents, parents, aunts, uncles, brothers, sisters, wives, husbands and children is still very fresh. Few Jews are unscathed by the personal tragedies inflicted by the Holocaust.

This is no reason for Jews to ignore examples of genocide against other peoples. In that same Holocaust, millions of non-Jews were also slaughtered: trade unionists, intellectuals, gypsies, Marxists, homosexuals, political prisoners, captured enemy soldiers, etc.

Nor can we—nor must we—forget examples of genocide such as the slaughter of Armenians by the Turks in 1915 or the treatment by our own government of American Indians.

It is immoral and a blasphemy of the memories of all victims of the Holocaust and other holocausts to look upon this as a solely Jewish tragedy.

True, the world was silent, but that indifference was practiced toward all the victims, Jewish and non-Jewish.

Why didn't Jews fight back in the Holocaust?

They did; at least, some did. The stories of grim and gallant resistance in the Warsaw Ghetto and the ghettoes of Vilna in Lithuania and Warsaw and Lodz in Poland, and the record of Jewish underground fighters in the forests of Nazi-occupied Europe are a testament of heroism and bravery.

True, the majority of the six million Jews who eventually were annihilated in the Holocaust did not offer a significant resistance. The only explanation which makes any sense is that it is virtually impossible for an unarmed, starved and beaten group of human beings to mount an effective offensive against a superbly-armed and equipped group bent upon genocide, which is what the Nazis were.

There is an additional, and poignant, reason. Like all other human beings, the Jews of that era could not really accept the reality of the fate that was in store for them. The psychologists call it "internalizing." Until it was too late, they wanted to believe that they were being shipped to "relocation centers" and "work camps," rather than to the concentration camps and the gas chambers.

And the world was silent!

I belong to a country club which has the best clay tennis courts and golf course in my community. I love exercising in the plush environment. Recently, I invited a friend, who happens to be Jewish, to tee off with me on two occasions, a week apart. I have received a letter from the board of the country club calling my attention to the fact that I had a Jewish guest using the facilities twice within a short period and reminding me of the club rules which exclude Jews and Blacks. I was

vaguely aware of the club's policy but had never paid much attention to it. I am not anti-Semitic, but the few Jewish friends I have, including my golfing guest, say that the only way to prove that is to quit the club. What do you think?

Your friends are quite correct. Remaining as a member of the club means that you are giving passive assent to its exclusionary policies of racism and bigotry.

Since you asked, you should resign and accompany your resignation with a letter to the club's board of directors specifying why you are quitting and calling attention to the fact that keeping individuals or groups out because of religion, race, creed or ethnic identity is as out-dated as it is un-American.

You can join another, "non-sectarian" club in your community. Its tennis courts may or may not be made of clay, but, at least, its leadership will not have feet of clay!

16

A Potpourri of
Clues about Jews

Are there Jewish foods?

Not original Jewish foods. There are dishes which are considered
Jewish but which have been adapted and modified from the foods
of the peoples in Europe and the Middle East among whom Jews
have lived for centuries.

Among these mouth-watering, taste-tantalizing treats which you
can nibble, munch and chomp are potato *kugel* (our favorite), a baked
potato pudding; a carrot delight called *tsimmes,* and *hummus,* made
of smashed garbanzo beans and seasonings.

Bagels, dill pickles, potato pancakes and rye bread are some of
the other delicacies popular among Jews.

The "contribution" so-called Jewish cooking may have made to
national cuisines would be the addition of fats, salts and sugars.
This, in turn, has produced the cardiovascular and diabetic conse-
quences which, along with ethical considerations, have inclined
thoughtful Jews in the United States and the United Kingdom to
become vegetarians, a very appropriate step, because *Genesis 1:29*
tells us that God has given "every seed-bearing plant...every tree
that has seed-bearing fruit...for food."

The place to find the authentic Jewish food, then, is in the first
chapter of the first book of the Hebrew Bible!

Is it true that Jewish people are not permitted to hunt?

It's true. The 18th century Rabbi Ezekiel Landau said of hunting: "...this is not the way of the descendants of Abraham, Isaac and Jacob....It is an unworthy practice....It partakes of cruelty....It is strictly forbidden."

What makes something "kosher"?

(Read this answer from beginning to end; you are in for a surprise!)

The *kosher* dietary system is concerned with three things: the kinds of animals, fowl or fish which are permitted to be eaten; the manner in which they are slaughtered; and the way in which they are served.

The word, *kosher (KO-sher),* itself, means permitted, fit, proper. Its opposite is *trefa (t'RAY-fah),* a no-no.

Leviticus 11:3 in the Bible defines as permissable "any animal who has true hoofs, with clefts through the hoofs, and who chews the cud...." An animal who meets two of the three requirements isn't acceptable; all three must be present. So, cattle, sheep and goats are O.K. Swine, camels and rabbits are out.

Leviticus goes on to define fowl that are *kosher:* chickens, turkeys, ducks and geese, pigeons and squab. On the other hand, wild birds, birds of prey, are *trefa.*

Fish that have fins and scales are O.K. Those that don't—lobsters, crabs, oysters, shellfish, eels, for example—are out.

The animals and fowl which are acceptable must be slaughtered according to precise rules by a Jewish ritual slaughterer. When the carcass gets to a *kosher* butcher, he must rid it of all blood by removing the major veins and arteries. Finally, at the butcher shop or at home, the meat must be soaked in water and salted.

Meat and dairy foods must not be served or eaten together at the same time. The separation of meat and dairy products extends to the dishes and utensils on which they are served or with which they are eaten.

Orthodox and Conservative Jews believe that the *kosher* dietary laws are of divine origin and must not be violated. Reform and secularist Jews usually do not observe the dietary laws.

The idea of keeping *kosher* has centered around eating animals. There are an increasing number of Jews—the authors of this book included—and others who reject eating animals, for ethical as well as health reasons.

Vegetarianism, they and we believe, is the ultimate in *kosher* practice!

Why do you claim that "vegetarianism...is the ultimate in *kosher* practice"?

Vegetarianism carries us a giant step forward into the ideal world, the Messianic Age.

In Isaiah's description of the ideal world, we find that "...the lion, like the ox, shall eat straw....They shall not hurt nor destroy in all My sacred mount." *(Isaiah 11:7,9)*

Esteemed Jewish commentators such as the Ashkenazic Chief Rabbi of pre-state Israel, Avraham Isaac ha-Kohen Kook, have pointed out that peace on earth begs for peace between people and animals.

The revered Rabbi Kook, a committed vegetarian, stated that "no one shall hurt or destroy another living being."

The great Jewish philosopher and physician of the Middle Ages, Maimonides (1135–1204), pointed out that Judaism forbids causing pain to any animal. The thousands of Jewish Vegetarian Society members in Israel, England and the United States agree.

They join the millions of vegetarians in the world who believe that vegetarianism can help alleviate world hunger. The world's land resources should be used to provide grains, vegetables and fruits for all, instead of being ravaged to raise grain which is fed to animals who, in turn, are slaughtered to feed meat-eating human beings.

"For the Lord your God is bringing you into a good land...a land of wheat and barley, of vines, figs, and pomegranates...a land of olive trees and honey; a land where you may eat food without stint...." *(Deuteronomy 8:7, 8, 9)*

Topping the list of the most famous Jewish vegetarians are two Nobel laureates in literature, Isaac Bashevis Singer and S.Y. Agnon, as well as the legendary Franz Kafka.

Kosher means "fit" or "proper." A much more humane as well as delicious and healthy diet can be followed without the torturous cruelty involved in raising, transporting and slaughtering feeling creatures.

I have heard that Hitler was a vegetarian. True or not?

Hitler was not—repeat, not—a vegetarian.

In a letter to the authors of this book, Philip L. Pick, spokesperson for the world-wide, London-based Jewish Vegetarian Society, wrote: "In recent years certain Nazi circles in Germany have encouraged the statements that Hitler, and some other leading [Nazi] personalities were vegetarians and anti-vivesectionists in order to persuade world opinion that they were really humane personalities."

Mr. Pick reported that even when Hitler was treating his stomach ulcers with diet he partook of the lavish platters of extensive flesh foods he provided his generals at dinners.

As a matter of fact, Magnus Schwantje (1877–1959), the author of *Moral Reasons Against the Consumption of Meat,* was banished from Nazi Germany for his views on animal rights and vegetarianism by none other than Adolf Hitler!

Hitler's close associate, Albert Speer, reports in his book that his *fuehrer* had a weakness for meat-filled ravioli and sausages from butcher shops in Munich. (Albert Speer, *Inside the Third Reich.* New York: Avon Books, 1971. pp. 74, 146, 154)

No, Hitler was not a vegetarian. But Susan B. Anthony, Albert Einstein, Albert Schweitzer, Gandhi, Tolstoy, George Bernard Shaw, Upton Sinclair, Voltaire, Rousseau and da Vinci were.

Is kosher slaughtering at least more humane?

Slaughter of animals and fowl according to the Jewish dietary laws is regarded as a religious act by traditionally observant Jews and is performed by a *shohet (SHOW-kheht),* a person trained in the many laws and restrictions which were developed in earlier centuries to reduce the trauma and pain of the animal's death.

As it is practiced in the United States, *kosher* slaughter involves the hoisting and shackling of fully-conscious animals before the actual killing, a practice which causes needless pain and suffering.

Humane groups have long advocated the use of holding pens for the positioning of the animals prior to the ritual throat-cutting as an alternative which does not violate *kosher* laws.

The bottom line is that there can be no "humane" procedure when slaughter is involved.

Is Hebrew the official Jewish language? Isn't there a language called Jewish?

Let's designate Hebrew as the classic, rather than the "official," language of the Jews.

Hebrew is the language of the Bible (what Christians call the "Old" Testament). It was the daily language of Jews until about 100 B.C.E. when it was replaced by Aramaic, a related Semitic language which had been brought to the Holy Land by the returnees from the Babylonian Exile.

Revived as a popular tongue with Jewish settlement in Palestine beginning in the last decade of the 19th century, Hebrew is today the language of the State of Israel.

Hebrew is also the language of the Jewish prayer book.

The language you call "Jewish" is *Yiddish (YIH-dish)*. It uses the same printed and written characters as does Hebrew, but it is a separate language. It arose in the ninth century C.E. in the Rhine Valley of Germany. It is a combination of Hebrew and medieval High German, together with many words taken from the language of each country where Jews lived. For example, Yiddish is spiced with Polish, Lithuanian and English words.

Just as Yiddish was spoken and read by Jews of European origin, a language called *Ladino (lah-DEE-no)* was the language spoken by *Sephardic (seh-FAR-dik)* Jews from the Iberian peninsula and the Middle East. It became popular after the Jews were expelled from Spain in 1492.

Ladino is a combination of Hebrew and Spanish, and it is seasoned with Arabic, Greek, Turkish, French, Italian and Portugese words.

If you are interested in knowing more about languages that Jews have spoken and words from those languages which are a familiar part of the English we speak today, you might want to read *The Jewish Word Book,* written by Sidney J. Jacobs and published in 1982 by Jonathan David Publishers of Middle Village, NY.

Is drinking allowed in the Jewish religion?

Drinking, within moderation, has been associated with Jewish religious observance from earliest times.

The Sabbath, Festivals and Jewish New Year are ushered in with the recital in the home and synagogue of the *Kiddush (KIH-doosh),* the sanctification over wine. The Kiddush, including a blessing acknowledging God as "Creator of the fruit of the vine," is recited before drinking the goblet of wine.

Observant Jews also recite the same blessing over the wine which they drink with lunch after synagogue services.

The Hebrew Bible speaks of "wine that cheers the heart of men." *(Psalms 104:15)*

The drinking of whiskey as well as wine is customarily accompanied by the familiar toast of *"l'hayyim (leh-KHAH-yeem)*—to life!"

At each *seder (SAY-dare)* banquet on the Passover festival, every adult imbibes four cups of wine as part of the ritual.

Certain Jewish holidays, such as *Purim (POO-reem),* which commemorates the escape of Persian Jewry from a governmental decree of death, and *Simhat Torah (sim-KHAHT toe-RAH),* the holiday of rejoicing over the Pentateuch, are also marked by drinking.

As you can see, consumption of alcoholic beverages among Jews was associated with ritual and holiday observance both at home and in the synagogue. Intoxication was considered inappropriate and vulgar.

Consumption of wine or liquor was done socially, because it took place in the context of family or synagogue observance of the Sabbath and holidays. The solitary drinker would have been an anomaly.

As a result, alcoholism and drunkenness were not considered Jewish traits. Jewish children, raised in this environment where alcohol was part of religious ritual and took place within the family circle, grew up without drinking problems.

In contemporary times, however, as American Jews have become thoroughly acculturated, alcoholism among them is on the rise.

Is dancing allowed in the Jewish religion?

Dancing is mentioned throughout the Hebrew Bible as part of religious ritual and to celebrate victories. Psalms 149 and 150 tell us that dancing and music were used to praise God.

Orthodox Judaism prohibits men and women from dancing together. As a result, at an Orthodox Jewish wedding, men will have their own folk dances and women theirs.

These restrictions do not apply to the other Jewish denominations.

On a recent trip to Las Vegas, I quickly became aware of the many Jewish comedians playing the clubs. Why are there so many Jewish comics?

Psychiatrists have known for a long time about the relationship between humor and tragedy. As far back as 1905, Sigmund Freud, who was Jewish, wrote a book on *Wit and Its Relation to the Unconscious*. This may be one explanation of why the Jewish people, whose long history has been marked by persecution and tragedy, has produced so many comedians in the Western world.

Not only Jews but members of other minority groups are very visible in the world of comedy entertainment. Perhaps, it is a way of subconsciously hitting back at the oppressive majority. Or, do Jews and other minorities crave acceptance through playing the court jesters and the buffoons?

Jews speak of their capacity for humor in the face of adversity as "laughter through tears."

Jews tend to be very verbal, and, aside from pantomime, comedy depends mostly on verbal routines.

I laughed my head off at a Woody Allen film last night. The movie was well peppered with references to rabbis and growing up Jewish. I wonder if Jewish people are offended by this kind of humor.

A portion of humor coming from members of minority groups is self-derisive and often borders on questionable taste when it is used to ridicule one's own group.

At that point, the question arises: Is it humor, or is it a manifestation of self-hate? Remember, in response to the previous question, we raised the possibility that Jews and other minorities crave acceptance through playing the court jesters and the buffoons.

When comedians who are of Jewish origin use Jews, Jewish religious practices or Jewish folkways in a tasteless fashion, they may be rejecting their origins, perhaps playing the clown to expose purported Jewish types or actions to the non-Jewish majority by way of pleading, "Take me. I'm not one of them. Look how I can outdo you in ridiculing my own!"

Members of the racial, religious or ethnic group may laugh at such humor, if it is really funny, but the laughter may be mixed with embarrassment and resentment.

Last Sunday evening, I attended a Jewish wedding. The invitation read 7:30. The ceremony didn't begin until 8:00. I was told this was "Jewish time." Do Jewish people have their own time?

That hurts! You've touched upon a vulnerable spot in Jewish behavior. Maybe, it's a matter of not wanting to be the first to arrive, so everyone comes a little bit late. A lot of little bits add up to a lot of late starts.

We have other faults, like answering a question with a question, as you may have observed on a number of pages in this book.

As far back as the opening portion of the Hebrew Bible, when God asks Cain, "Where is your brother Abel?" Cain comes back with "Am I my brother's keeper?" *(Genesis 4:9)*

So, back to your question, "Do Jewish people have their own time?"

Doesn't everyone?

Index

Clues About Jews for People Who Aren't
has been set in 10 point Century Schoolbook
and printed on 70 lb. Opaque Vellum at
Peace Press, Culver City, California

Design by Bonnie Mettler
Typesetting by Karen Mathews